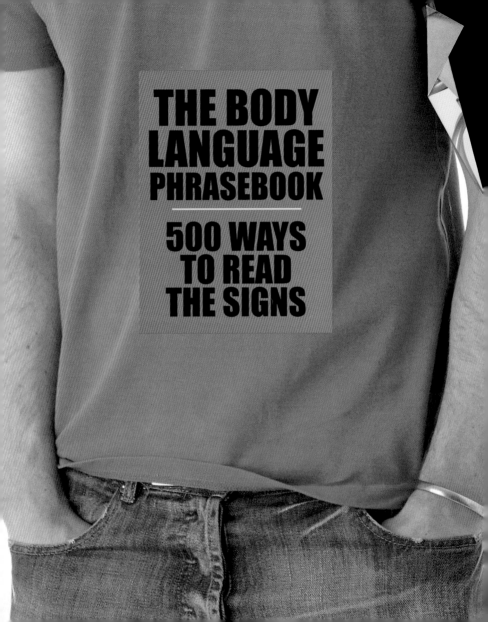

THE BODY LANGUAGE PHRASEBOOK

500 WAYS TO READ THE SIGNS

THE BODY LANGUAGE PHRASEBOOK

500 WAYS TO READ THE SIGNS

Nick Marshallsay

COLLINS & BROWN

First published in the United Kingdom in 2005 by
Collins & Brown
The Chrysalis Building
Bramley Road
London
W10 6SP

An imprint of Chrysalis Books Group plc

Volume © Collins & Brown Limited, 2005
Text © Nick Marshallsay 2005

British Library Cataloguing-in-Publication Data:
A catalogue record for this book is available from the British Library.

ISBN: 1-84340-304-8

Designed by Phil Clucas
Indexed by Sandra Shotter
Proofread by Andy Nicolson

Reproduction by Mission Productions
Printed and bound by SNP Leefung Ltd, China

Contents

Introduction

Awareness of body language and non-verbal communication has soared over the past few decades as people have become fascinated by the opportunity to both better understand others and also to change the impression they give to the outside world about themselves.

To varying degrees, we are all equipped with the ability to intuitively "feel" what someone is trying to communicate beyond what they actually say. Over and above their voice and words, we create this "feel" by assembling information from their gestures, posture, facial expressions, eye contact and movement. In *The Body Language Phrasebook* these indicators are referred to as clues. Why? Because one individual clue can rarely, if ever, be used to draw concrete conclusions. In fact, one clue can have many different meanings.

In this phrasebook, in most cases, just one possible interpretation of each clue has been highlighted.

People have sought out help and guidance about body language in order to attempt to "read" other people, to seduce the opposite sex, to sell something or to identify a liar. But great caution must be applied when trying to interpret body language and so this book should be read with five golden rules firmly in mind.

The five golden rules for reading body language clues and using *The Body Language Phrasebook*:

1 Never draw conclusions from one isolated clue. For example, raising your fist to someone is normally a display of aggression but, accompanied by a smile and a wink, is, of course, interpreted very differently. Look for groups of clues which point in the same direction. The more aligned and congruent clues that exist, the more likely they mean something.

2 Always consider local culture context and differences: The "OK" symbol of joining the tip of the thumb to the tip of the index finger can mean everything's all right in the US, however it has obscene meanings in certain parts of Europe! Be aware that some people from other cultures may also be modifying their behaviour to make allowances for cultural differences.

3 This phrasebook, like others, should be used as a guide to target countries only: Although some elements are nigh on universal, it is better employed as a helpful guide for non-verbal communication for the English speaking countries of North America, the UK, Ireland and Australasia.

4 Always consider the environment in which you observe the clue: Imagine you see someone sweating, this could be a clue that they're lying, however it could just be a sweltering hot day!

5 What we send and what we receive – perception is the reality of communication: An example of a charge often made against interpreting body language is, "My arms are crossed because I'm comfortable, not because I'm defensive." Imagine it from the other person's point of view though. If defensiveness is how they interpret crossed arms, defensiveness is what you will have successfully communicated.

Actions speak louder than words

- the power of gestures.

GIVEN THAT NON-VERBAL COMMUNICATION CAN OFTEN PROVE MORE CRITICAL THAN THE WORDS SPOKEN, it's no surprise we've developed a multitude of gestures to help get the message across. In this area cultural differences are particularly relevant – remember the second golden rule! The gestures in this chapter are our most consciously employed uses of body language.

NO WORDS NEEDED... MIMES

WHEN USING MIMES OUR HANDS INTERACT WITH IMAGINARY OBJECTS OR PEOPLE. SOMETIMES WE JUST DON'T NEED TO SAY ANYTHING AS GESTURES SEND THE WHOLE MESSAGE.

1 Bill please!

Whether it's for the check in the USA or for the bill in the UK, miming writing on the palm of one hand to a waiter makes a clear signal across a noisy restaurant.

2 Cut

It can be a threat, but rather less menacingly, the cut-throat gesture is employed to signal an end to an activity such as the shooting of a scene by a film director.

3 Mine's a pint

You look across a long table in a crowded bar and know you won't be heard, but you still know how to enquire if your mate wants a pint. Often topped off with enquiringly raised eyebrows and tilting of the head.

What did you say? 4

Perhaps at a noisy sporting fixture, in a loud nightclub or to encourage a rather softly spoken child, this gesture is quickly understood. Whether it actually helps in hearing what's being said is highly debatable!

5 Bang, bang

The index finger and thumb still symbolize "gun" from our time as kids playing cowboys and indians. As adults it may be office gossip over who's next to be fired.

Yeah, yeah, yeah, you're all mouth 6

… and no trousers. You've heard it a thousand times before, but nothing ever changes. Let your tormentor know they're all talk by mimicking their jabbering mouth with your hand.

7 Where is it?

Like a hammed up scene from a silent movie, the hand shielding the sun from your eyes signals you're looking for something.

8

Bedtime

Show me the way to go home, I'm tired and I want to go to bed. A simple way to say "sleep" without words.

9 Get me a cigarette

As you're standing at a crowded bar your friend places their index and middle fingers to their mouth, takes a drag and raises their eyebrows. Rather than a new nicotine-free habit, it's merely a request to buy a packet of 20 cigarettes without having to leave their valuable seat.

Phew **10**

What a relief. Usually employed when you've just escaped from a close scrape, you wipe away nervous perspiration.

11 I'll kill him!

Hopefully deployed in jest, we pretend to wring a neck to signal our extreme frustration with someone that we'd "like to throttle".

What a stink

As a mimic of preventing an odour getting up the nostrils, this gesture quite simply indicates a bad smell. It is often made with a screwed up face to indicate displeasure or disgust.

That's sick making

When something is just too nauseous or sickly sweet to handle, we mime the action of making ourselves vomit by putting our index finger into our mouth.

It's for you

Thumb to ear, little finger to mouth, miming a phone call can tell someone they're wanted on the line.

Have you got anything to eat?

This gesture can be used universally to indicate that you're hungry.

SIGNPOSTS... WHERE TO GO

WORKING OUT WHERE TO GO IS A MUCH MORE VISUAL THAN VERBAL ACT. BY USING GESTURES, YOUR DIRECTIONS WILL BE MUCH EASIER TO FOLLOW.

16

Come over here

Probably the standard way for adults to call each other over to look at or to join in with something is to curl over our fingers.

17
Come here little boy

The index finger beckon is often used with children and reminds them of scary fairytale characters such as the witch in *Sleeping Beauty*.

 **Over here, now**

Beckoning someone with a jerk of the head indicates a degree of superiority or disdain as the caller doesn't trouble themselves to use their hands.

 **Our hands have minds of their own:** We may not be conscious of just how much we gesticulate as we talk, but we have learnt that we are more convincing, interesting and dynamic if we move our hands to reinforce what we say. Even when we're not in face to face situations, we seek ways to engage with others. Just watch the hands of someone on the phone during an emotionally charged call; even though they can't be seen their hands go wild.

Let's split

Husband and wife have been stuck at a rather tedious dinner party for over five hours; he catches her eye and points his head in the direction of the door. This is the head point, usually deployed as a covert device for indicating direction or intent.

20 Advance

When directing traffic, police need to leave drivers in no doubt as to their instructions, otherwise the result could be disastrous. To signal clearly they use this unequivocal beckon, using the whole forearm to invite traffic onwards.

That way

Showing direction is normally performed with an open hand, whereas if we want to indicate a precise item (not a person, unless we wish to accuse), we normally use an extended index finger.

22 Hop it!

In line with its role as the power or authority digit, the thumb point is usually used as a directive to order someone away.

ILLUSTRATORS

ILLUSTRATORS ARE THE VISUAL AIDS OF NON-VERBAL COMMUNICATION. ALTHOUGH NOT AN EXACT MIMIC OF THE ACTIONS, THE HANDS OUTLINE OR POINT TO ILLUSTRATE THE MEANING, LIKE A HUNGRY DINER PATTING THEIR STOMACH IN ANTICIPATION OF A GOOD MEAL.

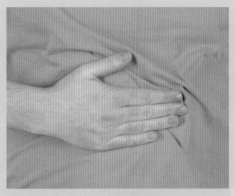

I'm hungry 23

Just as we feel hunger in our stomachs, this belly pat or rub simply makes a visual point to non-verbally communicate our need for a top up.

24

She'll scratch your eyes out

When mocking or exposing "catty" gossip or behaviour the fingers can be used as mock claws, scratching the eyes out of the subject.

25 Turn it down!

When it's too loud or you want to
show you're just not listening,
this gesture can be useful for saying,
"Turn it down!"

I've had 26 enough thanks

Placing a hand over the top of
our glass indicates we've had
enough to drink. It's a pity we
don't know how to use this
gesture more often!

27

Time up

Patience has run out; they've just gone on for too long and you certainly let them know it by tapping on your watch face.

28

Itsy bitsy, teeny weeny

This gesture signifies very, very small and is often made with the head craning forward and eyes squinting as if to pick out tiny detail.

29 It was this big

Loved by fisherman to exaggerate the size of "the one that got away" when referring to a freak sized catch that somehow escaped them. Whether accurate or not, this gesture is an ideal visual aid to communicate size to others.

30

Whatever

A relatively modern development originating from the USA, "whatever" is abbreviated argot for a sarcastic, "Whatever you say is right."

31

With all my heart

To show that what we are saying is meant with the full force of our emotions, we strive to physically link it to our heart. This has been formalized in the USA during the singing of the national anthem or when pledging allegiance the flag.

32

Hook 'em horns

Texan George Bush uses this gesture when alluding to "steer". It is also associated with the American Football team from the University of Texas at Austin. Beware in Italy... it signals to another man that someone is getting intimate with his wife!

33

You're crazy

Tapping your temple with your index finger alludes to giving yourself a lobotomy. It says we think someone has got a screw loose.

34

Get it out of my sight

Like a celebrity chef sending a poor excuse for a soufflé to the pig bin, disdainfully flicking a hand away with just the fingers from vertical to horizontal bids a person or object out of sight.

Show me the money

Rubbing the fingertips with the thumb signifies money. It may be indicating that yes, you can have something but you're going to have to pay for it.

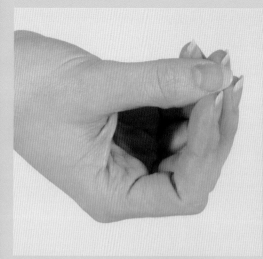

36

Here is my business card

In Japan a whole ritual is attached to handing over a meishi (business card), including handing the card at chest level, name showing with the index and thumb of both hands.

SYMBOLS

CULTURAL SYMBOLS HAVE BECOME GESTURE SUBSTITUTES OR SIGNALS WHICH HAVE MEANINGS WE ALL UNDERSTAND. TAKE THE SHOULDER SHRUG; WE ALL KNOW WHAT IT SAYS BUT IT HAS NO DIRECT VISUAL CORRELATION WITH ITS MEANING.

37 Yes

Surely one of the simplest and most widespread universal symbols, the nod has its roots in an act of body lowering, symbolizing acquiescence to the other party, giving in, or agreeing to their intent.

38 No

… means no when you shake your head. But why? One theory is that it is reflects a child turning its head from an offered mother's nipple first one way then the next.

39

Ummm, maybe

The hand waggle has several connected meanings depending on the context, from "maybe" through "I don't exactly agree with you" to "perhaps one solution, perhaps the other".

40

Not this Friday, NEXT Friday

By visually representing timescale, your interlocutor can see the difference from your finger leaping over the hurdle of this Friday.

Naughty, naughty

Accompanied by a verbal tutting and a pushing forward of the neck, we waggle our index fingers from side to side to berate or to chide. The index finger represents a metaphorical stick with which you are threatening the guilty party.

I know best

Employed with a knowing smile, the nose tap in the UK says we are clever, cunning or have the know-how to deal with the situation.

43 I dunno

Just the shrug of the shoulders alone is normally enough to signify "I don't know", but is often accompanied by the hand shrug and turned down corners of the mouth.

44 Fingers crossed

What we do for luck or, as children when telling lies, to protect us. This fingers crossed sign is a physical allusion to the Christian cross.

45 Power to the people

This power salute is a simple show of the fist and is beloved by revolutionaries as a symbol of resistance.

46

Cross my heart and hope to die

The self cross is likely to be derived from an ancient self curse signifying that if the speaker is lying then let their heart be cut in four!

47 Touch wood

"I've never had to go to hospital, touch wood." Still used today, touching wood is derived from ancient pagan traditions of worshipping the oak tree.

48 In the name of the Father, and of the Son, and of the Holy Ghost

Crossing is a centuries old custom of putting the fingers of the right hand to the forehead, to the breast, and then to the left and right shoulders.

Halt 49

The policeman standing in the middle of the crossroads, arm straight ahead, palm vertical, leaves you in no doubt you're going nowhere.

50 Timeout

Originating in North American sport as a call for a "timeout", it is now used more widely as a call for a break or a pause.

51 We will be victorious

Made famous by Sir Winston Churchill during the Second World War, it has grown in global usage to represent the struggle for victory, often more potently than words. It was also later turned against war as a 1960s' peace symbol.

Gimme a ride

Easily recognized and understood at roadsides in the UK and North America, be careful using it in some Mediterranean areas where it can be an obscene gesture!

Bad outcome

Nowadays representing a negative outcome, the thumbs down had more severe consequences for ancient gladiators. The thumbs down from the crowd signalled the downward thrust of the winning gladiator's sword into his prostrate victim.

Good outcome

Where thumbs down represents the negative outcome, thumbs up lets others know things have gone well.

Okay

Normally there are two clear meanings depending on the accompanying facial expression. Accompanied by a smile it means everything is good or all right. However, accompanied by a sad or disappointed look, it says "a big fat zero". Watch out with this one abroad though as its connotations can be obscene!

56 Under the thumb

When a group of men want to mock one of their number for compliance to the wishes of his wife or girlfriend, this gesture accuses them of being "under the thumb" or at the mercy of the will of their partner.

57

Yeah, right

By literally going "tongue in cheek", we sarcastically feign seriousness when actually joking. It originates from the act of biting the tongue to suppress laughter.

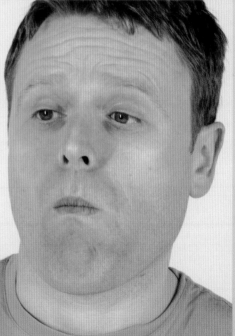

58

I've got it

Finger clicking: A brilliant idea flashes to your mind or you remember a fact that was eluding you – Eureka!

59

Delicious

Like an Italian man tasting the tomato sauce of his mamma, this gesture of kissing the fingertips, then pushing them away, says it couldn't taste better.

PUBLIC SPEAKING GESTURES

POLITICIANS ARE AWARE OF THE IMPORTANCE OF PUBLIC SPEAKING GESTURES AND SOMETIMES APPEAR TO BE OVERCOACHED. EVEN IN DAY TO DAY CONVERSATION WITH FRIENDS IN A BAR, OUR HANDS ALMOST ALWAYS MARK THE RHYTHM OF OUR WORDS, SOMETIMES DELIBERATELY, BUT USUALLY BECAUSE IT COMES NATURALLY.

I have nothing to hide nd I ask for your support

60

Showing the palms means the speaker is appealing to the audience, asking for their support and has nothing to hide.

61

I have achieved this goal and will hold true to it

The closed, upwards facing fist in front of the body symbolizes a goal reached, whilst leaving it in front of the body indicates the speaker will resist challenges and setbacks to holding their gains.

I'll take the 62 middle of the road

This softened fist with the thumb running along the side of the index finger conveys none of the strength, authority of a closed fist, nor the listening of the open hand. It's the gesture for the middle of the road speaker… a favourite of Tony Blair.

63 I will seize the opportunity to achieve this vision

By seizing the air, the speaker is metaphorically grasping at a vision for the future. Perhaps he is a politician articulating a goal or target which their policy will deliver.

64 I want us to understand and connect with each other

With the fingers spreading out root like towards the audience, the speaker is attempting to connect with them, to close the distance and join them physically.

65

I will cut through these obstacles

The hand chop seeks to cut through challenges, barriers or other confusion to arrive at a desired outcome.

66

I've heard enough

As if the palm is going to hold up or halt the flow of words from the audience, like King Canute attempting to arrest the rise of the tide, the speaker wants to stop the onslaught; they've heard enough and want to reply.

67 This is the way it is

Gesturing with the palm down is generally associated with authority and directing behaviour. The speaker wants no further contribution from his audience apart from listening.

I embrace you to join with my ideas

68 With this gesture, a speaker is trying to embrace the audience, to draw them in to their way of thinking, to bring them into the fold so that they can receive the collective protecting influence of the speaker and their ideas.

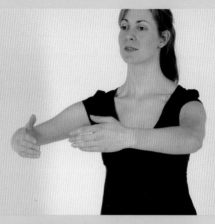

Let us join together

When the speaker may have a different opinion to the audience they employ this gesture to attempt to physically bridge the distance between the two points of view.

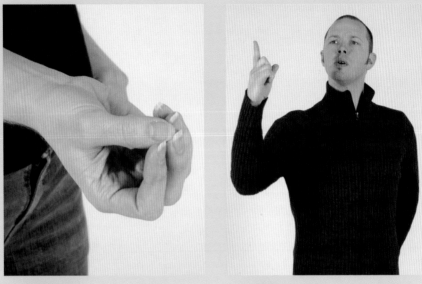

70

I will take care to get this right

By adopting the precision grip the speaker attempts to show how they will attend to the smallest detail and can be trusted to get things 100% right.

71

You'll be hurt if you don't listen

The index finger is waved high, as a stick. Its intent is perhaps to threaten the audience, or to reinforce to effect of the words and the implications of not listening.

72

I mean it, man

Rappers frequently mark out the rhythm of their song or drive home the impact of each line with the thumb and finger point, which at the same time may be a metaphorical pistol firing lines of prose.

To convey enthusiasm gesture a lot! People associate frequent and expressive gesturing with enthusiasm. Even though a speaker may be saying "I really believe this" or "I'm so excited", inanimate hands may give away their real levels of engagement, or certainly give their audiences that impression.

Say hello, wave goodbye.

HOW WE GREET PEOPLE AND HOW WE PART

from them reveals a huge amount about how we feel about them, our relationship with them and our relative status. On meeting any new person we rapidly form an initial impression based on what we see, hear and feel.

ACKNOWLEDGING SIGHT

WHEN WE FIRST CATCH SIGHT OF SOMEONE WE FEEL THE NEED TO GAIN THEIR ATTENTION, SIGNAL WE'VE SEEN THEM AND OFTEN MAKE A PHYSICAL GESTURE WHICH SAYS, "I'M CLOSING THE DISTANCE BETWEEN US."

73 I see you

When making visual contact with others we seek to reduce the distance by reaching out to them. This acknowledgement of the open, empty palm shows the absence of a weapon or other threat. It is the gesture opposite of a fist.

I can't wait to embrace you 74

Open arms when greeting someone is an attempt to close the distance and leave the body core open and exposed, inviting the other person into an embrace.

75 Thank you, my subjects

The British Queen is perhaps the only person we see waving with the back of the hand. This symbolizes authority and command as befits a head of state. Who else would wave like this in a serious context?

76 Sir!

The salute has been developed into a ritualized military recognition of an officer's rank. Although sometimes attributed to the raising of a visor of a mediaeval helmet to reveal the face, it is more likely just a structured way of hailing or acknowledging superiors.

77 I wish I could kiss you

If we're prevented physically from closing the distance, we attempt to bridge the gap by blowing a kiss. For example, when bidding farewell at a departure gate, or when a star acknowledges and responds to adoring fans from the red carpet at a glitzy event.

78 Welcome

Whether we're conscious of it or not, when meeting someone there is a brief "flash" of the eyebrows. Look out for it next time...

79 Knock, knock

The door is open, yet you still knock at the door. Why is that? Normally if we knock and wait, we're meeting someone of higher status, we don't have the authority, or we don't feel right just strolling on into someone else's territory.

80 Thanks for the applause

In years gone by, a gentleman would raise a hat to a lady. Now it's most commonly seen when a performer or sportsman acknowledges the applause and acclaim of an audience.

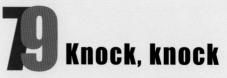

82 What's yours is mine

With a peer or subordinate we'll just wander on in to an office, we violate the territory without thinking twice about it.

Sorry to disturb you 81

Even more respectful and timid an act than knocking and waiting, some will feel so anxious about disturbing a higher status person that they'll just wait. At best they may scuff their feet or clear their throat to gain attention before entering. We fear to penetrate their territory without invitation.

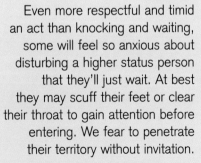

MEETING AND GREETING

BODY LANGUAGE PLAYS A MAJOR PART IN HOW WE GREET OTHERS. IT RANGES FROM THE STRICT FORMALITY OF THE BOW TO MORE RECENT, BUT EQUALLY RITUALISED GREETINGS OF POPULAR CULTURE.

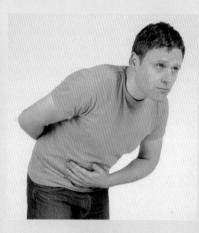

83 Honoured to meet you

These days we associate bowing either with some Asian cultures or extremely formal settings, such as with European monarchy. With the exception of play acting and mocking others, it's likely that most of us will never use the bow.

84 M'lady

Rather like bowing, the curtsey is an anachronism in modern culture. A form of body lowering, it may still be found as part of old etiquette displays, such as formal state occasions in the presence of royalty and certain formal dances.

85 It's not wort standing up

Sitting to greet someone: If you remain seated when introduced to someone standing it's either a really relaxed setting, or you just don't consider the other person sufficiently worth getting up for.

86 I'm stronger than you and I'm the dominant one here

The "crusher" handshake: We've all met them. Normally a man of advancing years who was raised with macho values… he who shakes hardest is the toughest. Nowadays all it conveys is a bully like nature of someone who sees dominating as their best way to get on.

I'm going to lead this relationship

One of the horror techniques taught by 1960s' sales courses was the 'I'm on top' handshake where you would seek to turn your hand so that you were palm down and metaphorically had 'the upper hand'. This should be avoided at all costs!

I feel awkward about shaking your hand

Be careful of jumping to conclusions about someone with a very limp handshake; there may be some medical or physical reason behind it. If not, this person may need some friendly advice about the weak impression it creates and the unease it may make others feel.

Sorry to put you to the trouble of meeting me

By leaning into the handshake you'll be offering the other party a minor act of body lowering, almost a mini-bow. To avoid this small act of submission just remain upright.

How do you do?

As the crusher handshake has been left in the dark ages, a firm handshake along with comfortable levels of eye contact is the correct way to greet a stranger warmly, yet confidently. As there is no additional body contact this is the most formal of everyday western greetings.

91 I'm really pleased to see you

The first step to reducing the formality of a handshake comes with the addition of a second hand. Each progressive demonstration of intimacy needs to be added with caution otherwise the other person may think it's just being done for show, or is over familiar.

92 This is more than just a business or formal relationship to me

As with the handshake and forearm hold above, the intimacy of the greeting is increased as the second hand moves up the arm.

I'm here to support you

93

In the correct situation, adding the elbow hold to a handshake can indicate that you are supportive of the other person.

94

I'm glad you're here

Now the second hand comes to its closest point to the vulnerable head and touches the body core in the form of a shoulder hold. It begins to show a caring and protective position.

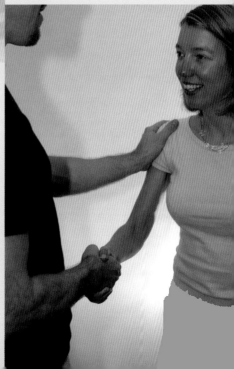

95 Pleased to meet you

By putting the caring arm around the shoulder you are offering protection in the same way as a parent, whilst offering the intimacy of your face close to theirs.

96

Great to see you old friend

This is the most intimate of handshake greetings, where not only is the hand shaken but maximum body area contact is achieved at the same time with the embrace. It is intended to convey warmth and liking, whether real or faked.

 Good to see you

The kiss on the lips tends to be reserved for either infants or lovers; used in any other situation is probably inappropriate. The closest approximation to kissing on the lips is to plant a single kiss on the cheek, normally to the right.

98

Hello darling

Which way first when performing a double kiss? There is no golden rule; just get on with it. The double kiss is more European than North American.

99 Absolutely fabulous to see you

The triple kiss may be common in certain areas of continental Europe, but elsewhere tends to be reserved for media 'lovies', drama queens and pretentious show offs.

Fabulous 100 to see you darling

The air kiss: As the cheek kiss became increasingly emphasized and ritualized, it evolved into a kiss at some distance from the cheek – an air kiss. This may well be done for theatrical effect and accompanied with an exaggerated kissing noise…"mmmwwuhh".

101 Great to see you

Friends greeting each other may embrace to the waist but keep separated from the waist down… perhaps they just don't think it's appropriate.

102 Fantastic to see you

Probably the most intimate of greetings, the full body embrace achieves the greatest degree of contact, inclusive of the sexual regions.

103 Hang loose

A gesture local to Hawaii, where it is used to reflect the laid back approach to life found in the Pacific Islands. Its use is particularly common amongst surfers.

Yo man, gimme five

Most commonly seen in the US, the high five, where raised open palms are slapped together, can either be a greeting or a congratulatory gesture. When used as a greeting it can also be a pre-cursor to a much more involved and elaborate display or sequence of "moves".

 **Yo**

Most often seen in black cultures as a replacement for more formal greetings, the fists of the greeters' hands are bumped together.

COURTESIES AND ETIQUETTE

We LIVE IN CONSIDERABLY MORE CASUAL TIMES THAN OUR PREDECESSORS AND INFORMALITY IS BECOMING MUCH MORE THE NORM. EVEN THOUGH WE NO LONGER LIVE BY A WRITTEN BOOK OF RULES, WE STILL SOMETIMES OBEY AN UNWRITTEN CONSTITUTION OF ACCEPTABLE OR 'CORRECT' BEHAVIOUR.

May I? 106

Once considered gentlemanly conduct, opening and holding a door for a woman could now land a man in the hot water of political correctness, particularly at work.

107 After you

Old-fashioned etiquette would dictate that a lady or a person of higher status goes through the door first. The higher status person may still lead today, however you may wish to amend this to allow a shorter person to go first out of courtesy, as it can be intimidating to follow someone taller.

108 May I take your coat?

This action, which would be common courtesy in the course of a normal greeting, may deliberately be ignored during a competitive negotiation where the "host" wants to maximize the feeling of discomfort or unfamiliarity on the part of the visitor.

Please sit down 109

It was normal practice in days gone by to offer someone a seat. Men in particular would make way for women, the elderly or people of status. Now it tends to be reserved for pregnant women and older people in our own homes or situations of shared seating such as public transport.

Please, be seated

Sitting first: traditionally the person of higher status sits down first. However as both work and social occasions become less formal, this rule has been increasingly abandoned.

When people are grouped together, especially with those they like, they frequently start mirroring the body language and other aspects of their communication of others. This can easily be tested by yawning whilst on a bus or train and waiting for others to follow. By copying the general position of others (but not exactly!) we may be able to make others feel we are like them and consequently they feel more pre-disposed towards us.

BYE BYE

THE AMOUNT YOU LIKE OR RESPECT A PERSON IS DIRECTLY LINKED TO THE EXTENT TO WHICH YOU MAKE AN EFFORT TO SEE THEM OUT OR TO PROLONG THE CONTACT.

111 Thank you for your time

By backing out of a room you are showing more respect by making the effort to maintain eye contact and by not turning your back.

112 See yourself out

Remaining seated as someone leaves may show you don't accord the person enough respect or care to see them away, or you consider them of lower status. However, it could just be a reflection of an informal setting or environment.

13 I'm sorry you're going

Walking someone to the door as they leave shows maximum respect or care for visitors. It is made even stronger if the host operates a further duty of care by overseeing the visitor's departure from sight, as if chaperoning them to the horizon.

14

Bye

The side to side hand wave is the most frequently used way of waving goodbye and is another open palm gesture. Can you imagine waving goodbye with the back of your hand?

15

Bye bye

Children often wave by flapping their hands vertically. Men will rarely wave like this as it causes them to adopt a limp wrist which has strong postural links to the female gender.

Why non-verbal communication is so important: Professor Albert Mehrabian conducted experiments which indicated that words could account for as little as 7% of what is communicated compared with 93% communicated by the non verbal aspects including aspect such as facial expression and body language.

Good or bad, happy or sad.
THE TURNED UP
MOUTH
OF A
SMILE

or the turned down mouth of sadness may be the basic ways of indicating whether we like something or not. But there's more to it than that where non-verbal communication is concerned. Gestures, posture and movement can all communicate degrees of liking.

I LIKE IT

Happiness, liking and celebration. Here we look at how we let it show.

16 I'm happy

A genuine smile is easily identified by the extent to which the muscles around the eyes 'join in' to create the overall effect.

17 Bravo

The hand clap has become an almost universal default for showing appreciation of others. Amongst some there is a gender difference where women will clap using 'praying' hands, symmetrically brought together. Men however, tend to clap into the "hands grasped" position at ninety degrees to one another.

Well done 18

Often between men, the pat on the back offers congratulations. On more refrained fields of play, such as the cricket field, it's a common form of acknowledgement.

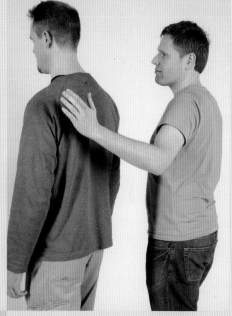

19 Good show, old man

When greater shows of intimacy and contact such as hugging just wouldn't be appropriate, correct male distance needs to be maintained, but when someone has done really well, back slapping is just the ticket.

120

Attaboy

In days gone by, shows of affection and closeness between men were shunned. Instead of an embrace to congratulate, which could be seen as soft, a more masculine solution of a mock arm punch praised the "chip off the old block".

121

Come on!

Now frequently seen on the tennis circuit by players such as Leyton Hewitt the fist pump is a pure show of aggression centred on man's key natural weapon, the fist. The photo of Muhammad Ali, standing over the vanquished Sonny Liston, brandishing his fist illustrates this perfectly.

122 Woo hoo!

Picture athletes as they celebrate success. Jumping for joy maximizes the possibility for a lone person to body raise over defeated rivals.

123

Take that

After scoring a goal in soccer, the most common form of celebration is to punch the air mimicking aggression or a knockout blow.

124 Go girl

Originally coming from a dance move this "go girl" gesture of two clasped hands making an exaggerated stirring motion has become a celebration ritual.

125

Yesssssssss!

Celebrating both hands raised: As with many forms of celebration, the key here is body-raising, where the individual attempts to gain maximum height in a display of dominance.

126 It's going to be mine, all mine

By slowly wringing your hands together at an angle to each other you convey anticipation that you're about to profit personally from something, perhaps at someone else's expense. Think of Gollum's "My precious" in *The Lord of the Rings*.

127

Cooooo-eeee

Whistling in surprise: You've just found out that you've inherited a rather large sum of money; as your eyes open wide you let out a long whistle, while slowly nodding.

I DON'T LIKE IT

DISLIKE, FEAR, DISGUST OR SADNESS…
THEY ARE ALL THE MANIFESTATIONS OF
SOMETHING WE REALLY DON'T LIKE.

I'm sad

Like the over-exaggerated make up of
the circus clown, by turning the
corners of our mouths down we signal
sadness. This is not surprising as it is
an upside down or anti-smile.

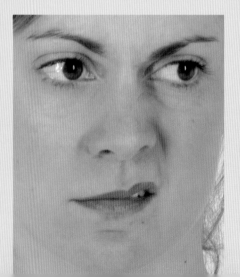

Grrrrrrr

The curled lip indicates dislike
or disgust and is an abbreviated
mimic of a dog baring its teeth
in a display of aggression.

Yuck

We signify disgust or dislike by wrinkling our noses. It's almost signifying an attempt to withdraw our nose from something that stinks.

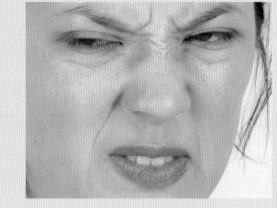

Uptight

Sitting with your body arranged in a perfectly symmetrical fashion displays a lack of relaxation and could imply you're not comfortable in your current situation.

132  Oh great

Typically the twisted smile is applied with a heavy dose of irony. It's a visual demonstration that we're unhappy and annoyed. However, forcing the sarcastically turned up smile says we're only putting up with it because we have to.

133

How do I get out of this?

Rubbing the back of the neck with your palm signifies frustration as we desperately seek a solution to the predicament we find ourselves in.

134 Feel sorry for me

Children are experts at using the jutting bottom lip as a negotiating tactic with adults to get what they want by appealing to our desire to look after and to nurture them. They are imitating a natural submissive reaction, unlike the lips pressed hard together which is usually associated with anger.

135

I'm going to cry

Quivering lips are often a precursor to crying. They represent the opposite of the hard set mouth associated with aggression and fighting.

136 Boo hoo

Love is closest to hate and, where crying is concerned, sadness is closest to happiness; just look at Olympic gold medallists sobbing on the podium or a cinema audience devouring tissues during a sad film.

137 Oh no

When things go really badly we attempt to physically block out the world, cutting ourselves off from the cause of our pain by putting our head in our hands.

ANGRY

WHERE SADNESS MANIFESTS ITSELF WITH A DEGREE OF PASSIVITY, ANGER IS OFTEN A FAR MORE ACTIVE EMOTION.

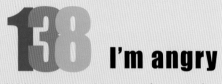

138 I'm angry

With the general bringing forward of the features of the face, the lips are pressed hard together and the nostrils flair as the temperature rises.

139

I'm so mad

When we're really furious with ourselves or something else we can't always stop ourselves from doing something about it. Instead we may be forced to take our anger out on ourselves, if only by biting our lips.

1**40** Doh!

Slapping the heel of a hand into the forehead is a form of self punishment. When we know we've been stupid and have only ourselves to blame, we use elements of self punishment such as this to take out our anger on ourselves.

How could I be so stupid?

When you're angry about something and it's your own fault, you can't always do something about it and are forced to pull your own hair out to release the anger.

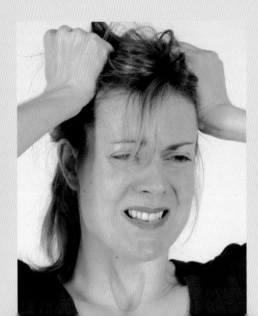

142

I can't believe it

Where a nod says yes and acquiesces to the opinion being put forward, when we throw our head back we are doing the opposite, dramatically raising our face in scorn and rage.

143

When sneering we bare our teeth as if about to bite. It is often accompanied by throwing our head back.

hat's below contempt

I'm so mad

The couple are off on holiday in the car, one is driving and the other is in charge of directions… and both are a little lost. As the journey goes on, the driver's hands gradually become more tightly clenched to the steering wheel.

I'm out of here

Storming out: When some people can't bare the frustration or anger of a situation any longer they theatrically storm out. It is a favourite tactic in negotiations and can be real or play acting. At home it's usually accompanied by slamming the door.

SECRECY

NON-VERBAL COMMUNICATION CAN INDICATE WE'RE KEEPING THINGS TO OURSELVES OR SHARING THEM WITH JUST OUR TRUSTED CONFIDANTS.

146 Between you and me

Known as the actor's aside, we use it to add secrecy when whispering to someone close at hand.

147 Our little secret

A wink is frequently accompanied with a small smile. It indicates a degree of intimacy between people as a shared or secret joke. The pleasure is in its understatement, confidentiality and as a souvenir of childhood.

148

I know the answer

This makes us think about school exams; rows of desks facing forward and closely arranged pupils completing the spelling test. And about preventing our neighbour from copying our answers!

Proximity: The emotion amplifier. We all like a degree of our personal space. Whenever possible, we maximize this, for example by sitting in the vacant seat on the bus. However, when we are forced into over-crowded situations, rather like other animals, minor provocations may ramp up our emotions where normally we may have remained calm. Just watch how tempers fray in the next packed subway or underground train you board.

149

Have you heard...?

When we whisper into another's ear we're sharing a secret that we don't want any one else to hear. We move close and almost make a physical bridge between us and our confidant.

150

Nudge nudge, wink wink

As in the classic Monty Python sketch, a knowing nudge at the elbow is a complicit encouragement to take some action about an opportunity that has presented itself. It physically pushes or cajoles the reluctant party into action.

Fight or flight.

4

WHEN FACED WITH A THREAT

man deploys his "fight or flight" response, through the body's release of adrenaline. This prepares him to either fight his way out of trouble or beat a hasty retreat. These responses have been key to man's survival.

AGGRESSION AND ATTACK

FORTUNATELY FOR MOST OF US, OUR DAY TO DAY LIVES INVOLVE LITTLE PHYSICAL CONFLICT WITH OTHER PEOPLE. HOWEVER, THE RELATED BASE INSTINCTS ARE STILL THERE, ALTHOUGH THEY ARE OFTEN FORCED TO MANIFEST THEMSELVES IN WAYS OTHER THAN STRIKING OUT AT AN ADVERSARY.

Attack face

An "attack face" is created by drawing the features together and forward, provoking an opponent and attempting to convey no fear. The lips may also be pulled back to bear the teeth.

Damn it!

One way in which we redirect aggression and anger is by releasing it against inanimate objects, such as smacking a table.

153 What are you looking at?

A typical show of aggression, raising the chin often brings us eye to eye with an opponent and demonstrates we're not afraid of exposing the throat. As with lots of dominant behaviours, it also has the effect of raising our overall size and height.

154 I mean business

Protecting the eyes is vital to man's ability to fight. By lowering the eyebrows the eyes are more guarded and may serve as sufficient warning to scare off a would be aggressor.

I'm going to crush this problem

When made angry at our everyday places of work we don't have the opportunity to physically punish the cause. Banging the table with our fist is an example of taking out what we would like to do to our competitors on an object.

Now I'm mad

Normally signalling aggression or anger, by flaring the nostrils man allows more air to flow making him more ready for the fight.

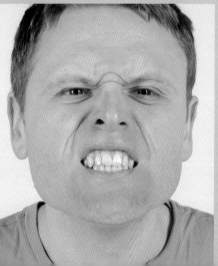

Come on then...

Folded arms with fists clenched conveys a highly aggressive attitude. The crossed arms are closed and confrontational, but the closed fists show the threat of a readiness to strike out.

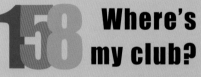 # Where's my club?

Newspaper rolling: Man triumphed as a species partly due to his ability to employ tools for mechanical advantage, with weapons amongst the most important of these tools. Nowadays people can frequently be seen rolling their newspapers in frustration, creating their own latter day club.

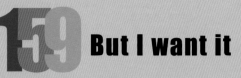

159 But I want it

One way of releasing aggression when we can't do so directly is to stamp our feet, like a sulking child denied a new toy. Although most of us grow out of this, it's sometimes still used by frustrated office workers.

160 I want to smash this problem

Glass smashing is another form of displaced aggression, where an inanimate object becomes the victim of our need to offload pent up aggression.

Try me for size

In this pose we are making a triple show of aggression, increasing our overall size by having our elbows pushed out, clenching our fists on our hips and making our posture square on to a potential aggressor.

I want to kick this issue into touch

When we kick something like a wall, a chair or a door in anger, the object becomes the embodiment of the issue causing us rage. It doesn't help solve the issue but certainly helps us feel better.

163 I'm going to beat this issue

Palm punching: In this case our palm becomes the problem that we metaphorically wish to defeat and we may make our point repeatedly by driving the fist into the palm over and over again.

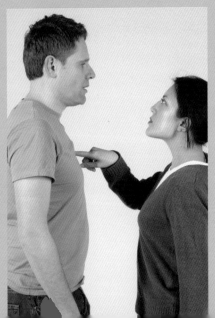

And 164 another thing...

We're mad and we're gonna let them know it. The index finger is turned into a weapon with which to attack our victim and we're going to get personal. By striking the body core rather than the arms we're moving more centrally into the other's personal space.

165

It's all your fault

Most of us feel pretty irritated when pointed at. It conveys considerably more aggression than the open hand when waved at someone. The index finger becomes reminiscent of a stick with which to threaten others.

166 I'm going to stare you down

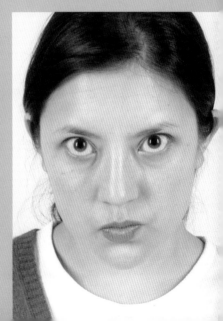

In western cultures typically we may look at someone for between 50 and 75% of the time during a conversation. Raising this to 90–100 communicates one of a few strong messages depending on the accompanying expression and clues. This could be aggression and intimidation, but equally we sometimes stare at those we find sexually attractive.

167 I'm going to stand up to you

Standing square:Whilst this makes a man uncomfortable due its links with fighting, women like to engage fully and directly with another person so they can read everything about the other and feel listened to.

168

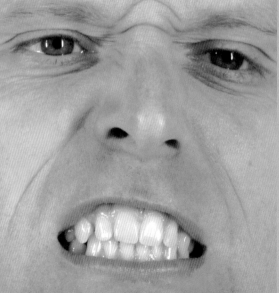

I bite

Baring teeth: The lips drawn back exposing the teeth to show our anger and aggression; this is a primitive throwback to the threat of the bite attack.

DEFENSIVENESS

TO PROTECT OURSELVES WE DEPLOY SEVERAL DIFFERENT STRATEGIES; WE CAN MOVE AWAY FROM A THREAT, MAKE OURSELVES LOOK SMALLER AND LESS THREATENING, OR WE CAN MAKE A BARRIER BETWEEN OURSELVES AND DANGER

169 I'm closed

One of the most commonly referred to clues of body language, folded arms are associated with defensiveness or being closed. It's always important to remember though that it should be viewed in the context of other non-verbal communication clues.

170

Don't look at me

With arms not as tightly locked as when folded, this position with parallel arms wrapped across the body enables us to cover and defend the maximum possible area of our torso whilst mimicking another person's hands holding us.

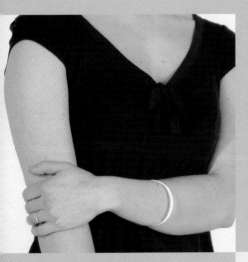

I'm looking out for number one

This clue is a combination of a defensive barrier of the arm across the body combined with the reassurance of a self hold.

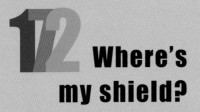 **Where's my shield?**

More frequently adopted by women, the hanging arm of this pose represents a defensive shield. The hand hooking onto the shoulder indicates this arm is going nowhere.

I feel a 13
little threatened

The cufflink adjust: One of Prince
Charles' favourites, this body cross is a
subconscious move to place protecting
arms across the vulnerable body core.
These days it is likely to be a response
to an intimidating social or work situation
rather than physical attack.

14

I'm protecting
my body

Similarly, by reaching across
our body to adjust a watchstrap
we're creating a barrier across our
front, reducing our openness and
revealing a degree of tension.

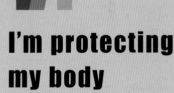

I'm protecting the important parts

With soccer players in a wall the need to adopt this "fig leaf" pose is obvious. However, many self conscious public speakers adopt this pose; their nerves make them feel vulnerable and for a man there's a really important area to protect!

I'm slightly protecting myself her

This pose is sometimes known as the "European Leg Cross", as North American men tend not to adopt it, deeming it effeminate. It is one of the most common resting postures. If linked with other closed clues it may point to defensiveness.

 **Convince me**

Legs crossed at feet: The further the feet are away from the body, the more the individual is indicating confidence by gaining "territory". This person will need some convincing as they are challenging the space occupied, but also being defensive.

18 Don't get me involved

By drawing back your feet under the chair, you're making your size smaller whilst reducing the space you take up. At the same time, balancing your feet on the toes reveals you're experiencing tension and may want to leave.

I want **19**
no part of this

Moving your feet underneath your chair reduces the space or "territory" you occupy. This suggests submissiveness and, combined with the defensive cross, indicates that you want to play no immediate part in the proceedings.

180

Leave me alone

This position, sometimes called "scissors", affords protection to the genitals, which could point to a feeling of insecurity. The individual may also be reassured by the comforting press of one leg on the other.

Keep your distance

A piece of furniture such as a desk can represent a barrier to communication in two ways. Firstly, it simply increases the physical distance between us and them, but also acts as a psychological shield.

182 I'm keeping my back covered

Most people feel more comfortable facing the room with their back to the wall. It is a natural reaction to want to see potential threats or risks whilst not leaving our vulnerable backs exposed.

183

I'm watching you

Imagine the teacher standing directly behind the naughty pupil at school. Someone out of sight but visible to others makes us feel distinctly uneasy as our natural defences tell us not to leave our backs undefended.

Help! 184

In *King Kong,* Fay Wray desperately holds her hands across her mouth when confronted by the giant ape. We do this when confronted with a major shock, surprise or horror.

185

Keep me out of this

Where we move towards things we like, the opposite is also true; we'll back off from someone or something we find objectionable or threatening.

186

I'm afraid of you

Crouching: Bended knees greatly reduce our overall size and may indicate a level of anxiousness and defensiveness as it prepares us to make a rapid exit from a threatening situation.

187 Bring me my armour

When reacting to a sudden stimulus our reaction is to withdraw and protect our head. By using a high collar or scarf we attempt to protect this vital area. This behaviour is often shown by soccer managers who sometimes seek to hide, almost child like, in the high collar of their jackets.

Size Matters: Man has created many artificial ways of making himself bigger and affording himself status when the body alone isn't enough. Just think of elaborate military helmets, such as the bearskin, bouffant hair displays, raised heels in men's shoes, padded jackets and suit shapes. All are designed to confer added height and power.

PANIC, FEAR AND FLEEING

THE DECISION IS MADE; THERE'S NO WAY WE'RE FIGHTING OUR WAY OUT OF THIS ONE. THESE CLUES INDICATE WE WANT OUT.

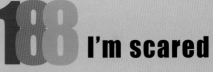 **I'm scared**

Whereas for an attack face the features are brought forward to intimidate, when we're frightened the opposite happens, we draw the face back as much as we can from the potential threat.

Leave me alone

When under extreme duress some people go back to the most basic defensive position – the foetal position.

190

Don't hit me

This defence mechanism is designed to afford maximum protection to the head. The hand, arm and shoulder are drawn around the head to create a protective helmet.

191

I don't want to look, but then again, I do

When something is too horrible to contemplate, we try to shut it out, but we still want to monitor the threat...just like watching a horror film.

Watch out

We have certain automatic reactions designed to protect us. When flinching we draw in our shoulders, and draw together our eyelids to protect the vital area of our head and eyes.

Ouch

When we see something unfortunate or painful befall someone else, we instinctively wince, simulating a flinch from the threat.

Protect me

When we are frightened we automatically grab at others to give us physical reassurance, just as a child holds onto a parent.

 **Duck!**

"Heads!" "Incoming!", the cry goes up on the sports field. Without having a clue where the ball is, the players' heads automatically go down. The reaction that has served us well over thousands of years still serves us well in keeping our heads out of harm's way.

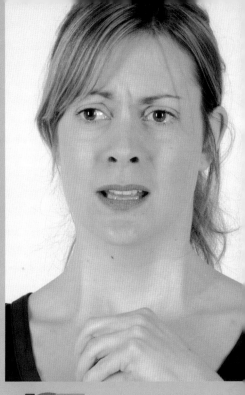

1**96**

I'm panicking

Rapid, heavy, short steps with
no clear direction indicate panic.
The person has overacted to a
stimulus in such a way that they
are no longer relaxed and to
some extent have lost control.

1**97**

Gimme air

As we feel a threat our breathing
rate rises, in an attempt to suck
more oxygen into our lungs to
prepare us to fight or flee.

Save me 198

In the wake of a natural disaster or other devastation, you will frequently see victims curled up in a ball rocking. They are shutting everything out to recreate the embrace and cradling of their parent.

I'm off 199

When we stand up out of a chair we place our hands on the armrests and use them to help push us up. We've learnt now that this simple signal alone, clearly says that we're leaving.

2OO

Where's the door?

By looking for the door our eyes are giving away our intent. As if searching for an escape route, we are making sure we know the quickest way out.

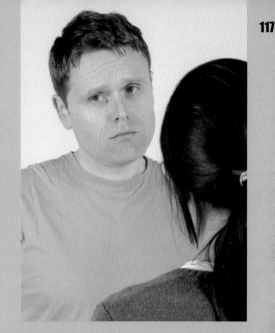

2O1

Get me outta here

Sometimes our desire to leave is so great our body will try to leave before our minds have made the decision for us. When someone is swaying side to side it may be the body is starting this move to get away, often it's due to discomfort with other people's attention on them.

SURPRISE OR CONFUSION

WHEN THINGS TAKE US ABACK WE FIND OUR REACTIONS HARD TO DISGUISE

What ?!?!? 202

The open mouth indicates surprise or confusion, especially when accompanied by wide open eyes and raised eyebrows. Watch someone who is clearly lost or looking for something; often their mouth is open.

203

What's going on?

When we are relaxed and our attention is drawn, we normally take our time to turn. But when a sudden noise demands more urgency, we rapidly turn our head to assess the nature of the threat and its urgency.

2**04** Really?

To show mild surprise we often lift one eyebrow on the side of the person making the comment. It is normally accompanied by a slight tilt of the head.

2**05**

I'm confused

We furrow our brow when deeply confused or worried. Hard to recreate after a serious dose of Botox! A furrowed brow indicates confusion, worry or exasperation.

INSULTS

STICKS AND STONES MAY BREAK MY BONES BUT GESTURES WILL NEVER HURT ME. EVERY CULTURE HAS ITS OWN FORMS OF NON-VERBAL COMMUNUCATION TO CONVEY INSULTS.

206 The poking tongue is associated with cheeky kids and could stem from a child rejecting its mother's nipple. Alternatively its origin as an insult may come from its power as a mimic for the penis.

Go away, I don't care what you think

207

You dick

Just think of Tom Cruise in *Top Gun*, giving "the bird" to the cold war baddy. The insult is a simple one… the stiff, straight finger being another direct substitute for the penis.

208

Kiss my ass

Many of the common modern insults have their origins in sexual references. When "mooning", the person exposes, without fear, their buttocks. Certain male apes will mount other male apes lower down the social order as a display of their dominance. When mooning we are mocking others by showing our disregard for such fears.

209

F**k you

This obscene gesture is relatively widespread and its implication is clear, the forearm a straightforward replacement for an oversized phallus.

210 Up yours

In the UK this means "up yours". It has been suggested that the gesture comes from the historical fact that the French would cut the first two fingers off captured English archers to prevent them ever fighting again. Subsequently, to antagonize the French prior to battle, the English archers would wave two fingers at the French.

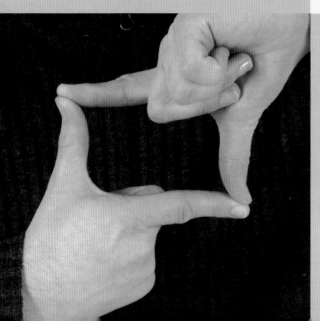

211 You're such a square

Originating in the USA this insult calls the target a "square", a reference to someone considered boring and conventional.

212 Loser

Born from the same stable of popular American youth culture as "Whatever", the victim is taunted as being a "loser" in life rather than just a sporting competition.

213

I spit on you

Spitting is a common form of insult. By spitting on the floor near a rival, the implication is that they are worthy only of your body's waste.

EXASPERATION

WHEN FRUSTRATION GOES SO FAR THAT IT CAN'T BE HELD BACK ANY LONGER, IT BECOMES EXASPERATION.

214 How tiresome

A heavy sigh indicates that frustration has become exasperation and is embodied by dropping the shoulders to a collapsed position.

How 215 frustrating

By blowing out the cheeks we exaggerate the action of exhaling, demonstrating our frustration.

26 Typical!

Signalling that you can no longer
bear to see what's before you, you
raise your eyes to the ceiling and
bring them down again quickly.

27

I give up

Throwing your hands in the air demonstrates you've been
pushed to the edge of anger. It can be viewed as over
theatrical and is commonly used by sportsman unhappy
with a refereeing decision, or by teenagers when denied
their parents' house for their 16th birthday party!

Master and servant.

AS MAN EVOLVED
ONE OF THE KEY
MECHANISMS
WHICH ENABLED HIM
TO BECOME THE
DOMINANT
SPECIES

was his ability to co-operate in groups. The key to cohesion within groups was the establishment of a pecking order or hierarchy. Although perhaps not easily spotted, clues to our status, relative to one another, still abound today.

DOMINANCE

Establishing a pecking order is all about establishing relative superiority with shows of height, size and power.

28 I'm the boss

This pose is rather militaristic or professorial. It conveys confidence bordering on arrogance, particularly when accompanied by a raised chin.

29

I've got the size to take this on

By puffing out his chest a man is making a basic size enhancing display intended to intimidate potential opponents.

I'm not afraid

Chin jutting: the prominent male chin is linked to testosterone levels and, when "jutted" forward, adds to the threat of the "attack face" where the facial features are drawn forward and together.

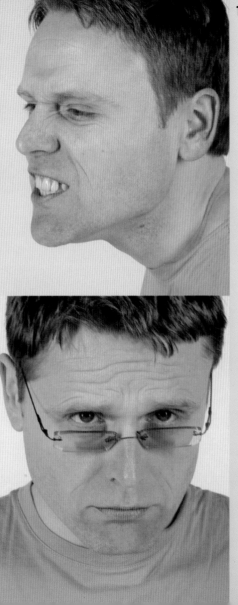

 **You're beneath me**

Looking over the top of glasses conveys disdain as it mimics looking down on someone and, when combined with a disapproving furrowed brow, indicates superiority.

222

I'm strong

As the thumb is considered the power digit, folded arms with the thumbs up is a straightforward show of strength. It is often seen in men's sports team photos. It has the additional effect of puffing up the biceps.

223

I'll lead you

The parent or adult places a hand on the shoulder of a child to guide them; in the same way this can be a clue that one adult is leading or guiding the other, or at least would like to be seen to be doing so!

224

Follow me

Like a boy scout leading an old person across the road, this is a guiding action where one leads the other by the elbow, a favourite of George W Bush when trying to be seen to lead other world figures.

225

I'm the authority

Lapel grabbing: This pose combines a number of authority and power symbols, which explains why it is employed by trial room lawyers and attorneys and police officers. The act of grasping lapels displays the power digits, the thumbs, whilst pushing out the elbows to increase the apparent shoulder width, boosts overall size.

226 I have a grip on things

When grasping a bar or railing, man employs the power grip where the whole inner surface of the fingers and thumb are wrapped around the handle – this still conjures up the primitive gripping of a weapon.

227

I'm big enough to handle it

This pose forces the elbows wide, making the person look bigger. At the same time, the thumbs are exposed and the hands may be in a typical "power grip" around the belt. A dominant, primarily male position.

I'm big 228

With our hands on both hips we are making a show of aggression or dominance by blatantly trying to increase our apparent size.

229

You're the tops

Dominance is all to do with size, height and perspective so to fete winning by raising the victor onto shoulders is no surprise. Just think of the immortal image of Bobby Moore, England's soccer world cup winning captain of 1966, as he was paraded on shoulders raising his arm and the trophy even higher.

230 There, there little girl

Parents lovingly pat children on the head, as much for the relative convenience of height as anything. To pat another adult on the top of the head is condescending in the extreme and reserved for playful mocking of good friends.

231 This way, I'll look after you

Guiding someone with a hand on their back may be done to give the impression you are leading someone else. A level of relationship should be established before trying this, otherwise it could be perceived as manipulative.

 I'll protect you

In some cultures (such as the Japanese) the back of the neck is considered a particularly sensitive body area. Even in our own we would need to have high levels of comfort with someone to allow them this privilege. Interestingly, footballers congratulating each other after a goal, permit this intimacy.

Here, the fists are shown as a potential threat in this pose, but additionally, the upturned elbows mimic a giant shoulder, growing the perceived size.

I'm pressing this point home

234 Strong and silent

By raising the thumb, the power digit, to the mouth we are bringing it to the centre of attention. This may well be a signal that we don't agree with what is being said and are signalling for the other person to stop talking.

235 I'm on top of this

By rocking onto the balls and heels of our feet we grow a few extra inches. This achieves the same thing as elaborate military helmets of old or "stack" heels on men's shoes.

236 I'm the leader

Napoleon is frequently depicted in this pose. It projected dominance by increasing his size but also showed he felt no threat and no immediate need to be ready for action, as his hand was tucked away.

237

I'm a cowboy

A classic cowboy pose. By standing with our feet wide apart, we increase our impression of size whilst displaying the crotch without fear of leaving it exposed.

238 You trust me

How many times is your head touched day to day by someone else? Unless it's a partner or close family member the answer is probably very rarely. As our heads are one of the most vital and vulnerable parts of the body, we know well to steer clear of getting this intimate.

239

Alert and ready

Sports teams often pose for a team shot with their shoulders back, chests out and hands on knees. Nobody wants to look the smallest person in the shot.

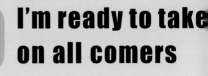

240 I'm ready to take on all comers

The cowboy swagger says we're always ready for a fight by making us look stronger and ready to swing a punch in a bar room brawl. Much used by George W Bush in his leather bomber jacket.

CONFIDENCE

Portraying confidence can be a major determinant of how we are perceived and the success we achieve. Wouldn't you like to be able to walk into a crowded room and convey bristling confidence?

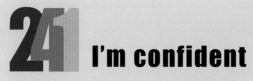

I'm confident

Raising the chin conveys confidence and a lack of fear. Soldiers are trained to stand to attention and look up, adding to an impression of fearlessness. However, raising the chin too far may convey arrogance and give the impression you are looking down on others.

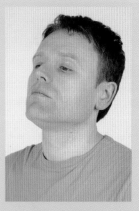

On an even footing

Having your feet flat on the floor shows relaxation and the absence of self consciousness. There is no "cross" or reluctance to occupy territory in front of you.

In control

Brisk purposeful walking, without rushing, shows no fear of what's ahead whilst the swinging arms and posture give size. This person is in control.

Well balanced

Feet planted shoulder width apart says this person is balanced and comfortable. They are relaxed yet ready for action if the need presents itself.

245 Even keel

Many people want to create a greater impression of confidence as they negotiate through work and social situations. A simple and quick win in this respect is the simple action of lifting the chin to a neutral position to show that you're ready to face up to whatever life throws at you.

246 Blowing my own trumpet

In a normal conversational setting, it would be rude to blow smoke horizontally into the group. By blowing the smoke up the smoker raises the chin and overall height, displaying confidence whilst not being afraid to bare the vulnerable neck.

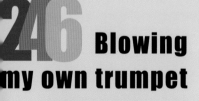

247

I'm at my ease

A real smile with the mouth closed portrays confidence by its absence of anxiousness. It conveys the impression that you are completely at ease with other people and don't feel intimidated. However, if it's held for too long you may look smug.

I'm up for it 248

Submissiveness is often equated with the body lowering actions of hunched shoulders and collapsed back. By simply drawing the shoulders back behind the hips we ooze confidence.

SUBMISSIVENESS AND LACK OF CONFIDENCE

MANY OF THE SIGNALS OF SUBMISSION ARE THOSE OF BODY LOWERING, MAKING OURSELVES SMALLER, LOWER OR MORE INSIGNIFICANT TO OTHERS. ALTHOUGH WE IMMEDIATELY THINK OF BOWING, SUBMISSION AND BODY LOWERING CAN MANIFEST ITSELF IN MANY DIFFERENT WAYS.

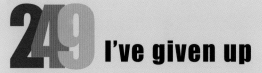

249 I've given up

The sunken chest draws down overall size as the back bows and the shoulders come forward and down making the person smaller. Originally this would have had the effect of making the person less threatening.

250 Despondent

A classic act of body lowering, the sunken chin reduces the perception of our overall height and averts our eyes. This lack of confidence symbolizes our submission to more dominant individuals. Just take a look at the losing side in a sports match.

251

Teacher and pupil

Normally when we are standing we feel more dominant. If we're sat at our desk and someone stands next to us it can make us feel downright uncomfortable.

252

I can't lift my feet

When a child is caught with his "hand in the cookie jar" and is being berated by his mother, his immediate response is stare guiltily at the floor and scrape the soles of his feet across the floor. Similarly, shuffling the feet when walking attempts to minimize our height.

253

m taller than I'm worth

Curving and collapsing the spine reduces our overall height. The spine frequently becomes more curved in older people, who again represent less of a threat.

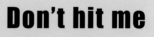

254 Don't hit me

By bringing the neck forward the head is lowered and our overall size reduced. It indicates lack of relaxation in a situation and conveys uncertainty.

255 I'm beat

Rounded shoulders: Dominance can be associated with broad shoulders, so by rounding the shoulders people reduce their size making them appear less threatening.

256

Back to school

You may have sat like this during 'assembly' at school with your legs crossed and heels drawn in. This sitting posture is rarely employed as an adult, perhaps because of its child like associations.

Feeling down

By blowing smoke down, the smoker is submitting to his or her audience by lowering the chin and eyes.

! Staring out: Subconsciously we may feel threatened by new encounters even if we don't recognize it. One way this may reveal itself is when people meet and shake hands. To avoid the confrontation at close quarters one or both may look away. On many occasions it may be the more submissive that looks away first.

2**5**8 I need to collapse

At the end of an Olympic final the athletes will often squat; the exhaustion has dragged them earthwards but they're still ready to move. Normally the winner is often doing the opposite, even when exhausted, with dramatic body raising displays.

2**5**9 I need to be careful

We use this precision grip when we take a fine hold of something. Although it doesn't convey submissiveness as such; it shows we're paying attention to detail.

POSSESSION & TERRITORY

MANY ANIMALS DISPLAY TERRITORIALITY AND MAN IS NO DIFFERENT. FROM MARKING OUT THE LIMITS OF OUR GARDEN TO THE WAY WE ARRANGE OUR DESKS AT WORK, WE ARE SETTING OUT OUR SPACE, WHICH IS NOT TO BE VIOLATED LIGHTLY.

260 Sorry!

Just as we are aware when our personal space is invaded, we're also conscious when we've invaded someone else's. If we accidentally bump into someone on the street we're quick to apologize and re-establish 'normal' operating distance.

261

This is mine

When a speaker spreads their arms out across a table they are trying to claim as much territory as possible. A clear display of dominance.

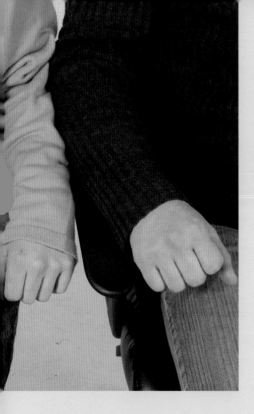

262

This is my territor

You're on bus, a plane or in the cinema. One armrest, two arms; a real chance to relive those testosterone laden battles for mates and territory just like your ancestors! Or, as close as you will get to it in the office world…

263

I'm master of the universe

If we rest our forearms and elbows on chair armrests we subtly increase the space we occupy, making ourselves look bigger.

264

I'm not that big

Timid or submissive people will keep their elbows tucked at their sides to make themselves look smaller, even when their chair is equipped with armrests.

265 No way out

By stretching our arm out straight we occupy the maximum area. We indicate that we are unconcerned by the other person's status as the posture indicates that we're quite happy to bar the exit.

266

Hands off

Although our friends in a bar are unlikely to make off with our bags or take a drink from our glass, we often rest our hands on them to mark our ownership.

267 That's mine

Just as we hold hands to indicate ownership of our partners, by physically resting our feet on our possessions we're stressing our ownership and hoping for the transferred effect of status. It also increases our apparent size and for a man, could be a crotch display.

RELAXATION

ACTS OF RELAXATION SHOW THAT WE HAVE NO NEED TO BE READY FOR ACTION. WE ARE NEITHER AROUSED, EXCITED NOR THREATENED BY OUR CIRCUMSTANCES. THIS MAY ALSO IMPLY DOMINANCE, SUPERIORITY OR LACK OF RESPECT AS WE ARE CONVEYING WE HAVE NOTHING TO FEAR FROM THOSE WE'RE WITH.

268 I'm feeling very relaxed

If both your hands are in your pockets, it's showing you're pretty relaxed. There is no one there of status or authority who warrants the respect of a more formal position, nor is there any imminent threat that you need your hands in a ready position to deal with.

269

I'm right at home

Arousal and excitement are often linked with being upright or even bent over towards the area of interest. By sprawling, you're moving away from these 'ready' positions.

I'm feeling **270** pretty informal

This is a very informal or relaxed pose, because you're effectively putting one arm out of action; you're not going to need it anytime soon.

271 I'm king of the world

Sitting with your feet on a desk show you're not about to go anywhere, you're also marking out your territory and that no one around merits formal respect. Its closeness to the horizontal position shows relaxation. Be careful of this one in certain cultures where exposing the soles of your feet is a serious insult.

I'm feeling 272 pretty informal

Sometimes called the figure four, this is the more common way of sitting cross legged in North America. It is considered more informal and relaxed in Europe. The horizontal lower leg can project a barrier between you and others.

273 I'm relaxed but not taking in what you're saying

This leg barrier in a figure of four can be highlighted by holding the arms out or hands hooked over the shins. The palms are down so the sitter is not looking receptive.

274

No cares in the world

Perhaps one of the most relaxed postures; we associate it with dreaming of a blissful Caribbean holiday. In this pose we leave ourselves helpless and open to attack as our core is exposed. This position shows we have no fear of such a threat and are completely comfortable with the situation.

275

No panic

Walking slowly conveys the fact that we're just not worried or panicked by our current environment. We're the one in control and are not going to be phased or rushed by external stimuli.

I feel at ease 276

Your level of arousal is low, the body is relaxed, devoid of tension, so much so that you collapse back in the chair.

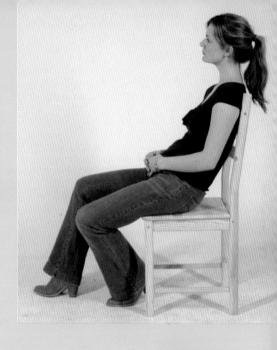

I'm the man 277

The swaggering walk is characterized by a slow roll of the body, chin up, chest out and shoulders swinging like John Travolta during the opening of *Saturday Night Fever*. The whole intent of the swagger is to both increase the impression of overall size and show relaxation.

278

I'm going to be here a while

The relaxation of leaning against a wall indicates that we are not ready for action and have no imminent plans for departure.

279

I feel right at home

Sitting with a leg over the arm of a chair is a clue of high relaxation and comfort. Whilst increasing size and territory occupied, you're also slouching and spreading in the chair with little concern for status. For men, it's also a crotch display.

280

I'll sit where I like

Sitting on a table can be used deliberately to convey informality. It's nearly always restricted to relaxed settings. Employees are unlikely to do this whilst holding a conversation with their CEO… they wouldn't dare take the liberty.

281

m feeling relaxed

If you are highly aroused or expect immediate action your hands are poised. By tucking one in a pocket you're projecting that you're feeling at ease.

Relaxed and on top of things

Tables are not designed for perching on. Parking your behind on a table infers a peer or superior relationship necessary to perch like this.

How territoriality drives posture: The way we sit or stand causes us to occupy more or less space. Frequently, assertive or dominant people will have no qualms about making themselves at home by spreading their possessions, extending their arms across the table and having their legs stretched far forward, claiming that territory as their own, just as surely as putting a flag on it.

283

I'm hanging around

Balancing primarily on one leg renders the stander less balanced and consequently more vulnerable. Their intent could well be to hang around; as their legs are "tied up" they are not in a position to act quickly.

284

Take it easy

If we're lying down we're feeling a very low degree of threat and high degree of relaxation. To react from this position is both tricky and time consuming.

The eyes have it.

AS THE SAYING GOES, THE EYES ARE THE WINDOWS ON THE SOUL.

Not only do we strive to make eye contact with people we're speaking to, at the same time we subconsciously read their intent, reactions and feelings through their eyes.

EYES WIDE OPEN OR CLOSED TIGHT SHUT?

THE SIMPLE ACT OF OPENING THE EYES WIDE OR CLOSING THEM TO A SQUINT SAYS A GREAT DEAL TO OTHERS.

Beady eyed

Studies have shown that when people are presented with images they don't like, their pupils narrow. If we observe the eyes carefully we too may be able to read these subtle indications of the reactions of others.

286
Wide eyed

In the same way that our pupils narrow when presented with an image we don't find appealing, we literally go "wide eyed" with dilated pupils when confronted by something we like.

 **Look after me**

We find wide open eyes attractive. This may be related to the wide open eyes of a baby, which arouses in us the desire to care for and protect them.

Oh really

If we raise both eyebrows and keep them raised it often displays surprise or interest. It increases the amount to which our eyes appear to be open.

Two sets of eyes

Why do people rest their sunglasses on the tops of their heads? Sure, it may be just convenient or may be keeping long hair back, but it still has a certain visual appeal. This could be because the glasses mimic a giant set of pupils, an image we find fundamentally appealing.

My, what big eyes you have

Studies have shown that we find dilated pupils attractive. Wearing thick rimmed glasses may subconsciously add to our appeal by creating a look of "super eyes".

291 I can't look!

Closing our eyes can be a very visible reaction to a frightening scene or it may arise as a more fleeting signal in the form of a prolonged blink as people attempt to cut off what they're seeing or momentarily escape from a tough corner.

I'm giving nothing away 293

Lee Van Cleef had shiftiness, cunning and guile off to a tee. Being the opposite of babies' wide eyes, narrow eyes may communicate suspicion, doubt or sneakiness.

292 Hiding something?

It is very telling that when we're talking to someone wearing sunglasses, we find the experience rather unnerving. Do I have their attention? Are they looking over my shoulder? How are they reacting to what I'm saying? The eyes often give this away. No wonder many serious poker players wear sunglasses.

EYE ACCESSING CUES

Neuro-Linguistic Programming (NLP), developed by Richard Bandler and John Grinder, suggested that you may be able to understand how a person is processing information by observing the way in which they glance when thinking. They suggested the way may be reversed with some left handed people and certain exceptions. This can be explored in the first instance with a few test questions.

Talking to yourself? 294

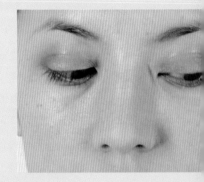

Looking down to the left: Here they are talking to themselves... for example, "Where did I put those keys?" or "Why do I always miss my backhand?"

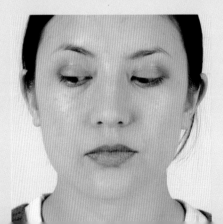

295 How am I feeling

Looking down to the right: When someone is considering their emotions, feelings and sensations they may look this way. This can be tested with a question such as "How did you feel when you saw your ex-boyfriend again?"

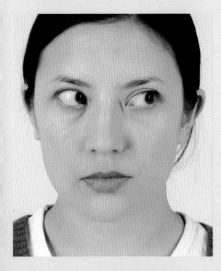

296

What did that sound like?

Looking to the left: When remembering a sound. "What was the music that was playing?"

297

What would that sound like?

Looking to the right: If you are imagining a sound, for example, "What would it sound like if you dropped a piano from the 20th floor?"

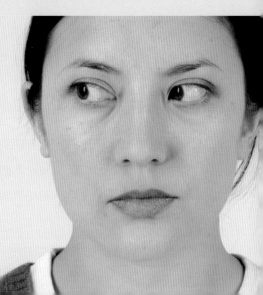

298

What did that look like?

Looking up to the left: If you're trying to remember what something looks like. You can test this with questions such as, "What colour are your bedroom walls?"

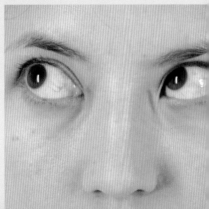

299

What would that look like?

Looking up to the right: Someone may look in this direction when they are trying to imagine what something may look like. "Imagine a blue dog on roller skates". Thus, when someone is looking like this, Bandler and Grinder suggest they are constructing rather than remembering something. However, don't use it as an amateur lie detector, as some have suggested!

THE EYES HAVE A LANGUAGE OF THEIR OWN, WHICH IS WHY MASKING THE STORIES OUR EYES TELL CAN BE NIGH ON IMPOSSIBLE.

300 How am I looking?

Humans have developed a considerable edge to assist themselves in the preening process… the mirror. The rest of the animal kingdom make their mating displays without the luxury of a self-image. Our desire to preen has even influenced our environment, when did you last go into a public washroom that didn't have a mirror?

301 You can trust me

Appropriate, comfortable levels of eye contact are associated with confidence, openness, trust and interest. We're not afraid to meet someone's gaze and are happy to have their attention on us.

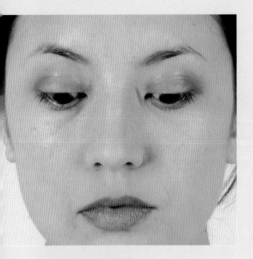

302

Don't mind me

Eyes looking down gives the impression of a lack of confidence, shyness and timidity. They avoid confronting or facing up to issues and are the eyes' version of body lowering, making the person 'smaller' and less significant.

303

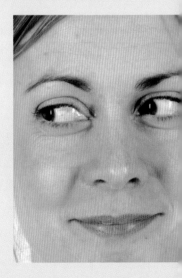

Over there

Eye pointing: Conscious or subconscious… If you want to point the way to someone with the minimum of warning to others, using the eyes could be the answer. Sometimes though, our eyes can give the game away. Staring longingly at our partner's left over french fries tells them we can't wait to help them clean up.

304 I'm guilty and I know it

Looking away: The classic "child caught with their hand caught in the cookie jar", we look down guiltily to avoid eye contact when we're getting a telling off. This submissive act can become a habit, undermining our ability to convey confidence to others.

305

I can't believe that's happened

Rolling the eyes: When exasperation has reached such lengths that we simply have to look away, we roll our eyes first to the ceiling and then down in a falling arc to one side or the other.

How interesting.

WHEN COMMUNICATING WITH OTHERS OUR DEGREE OF INTEREST OR ENGAGEMENT with what they are saying can vary enormously. Sometimes we're excited and enthralled by what we hear, on other occasions we either feign interest or resort to open shows of boredom.

INTEREST, LISTENING AND CONCENTRATION

WHEN WE'RE STIMULATED AND INTERESTED IT'S NORMALLY PRETTY EVIDENT, AS WE'RE ALERT, FOCUSED AND READY FOR ACTION.

306 I'm keen to listen to you

The head tilted to one side can be a clear clue that we are listening as it's the opposite of the aggressive head square on and straight. It also reminds us of a child leaning their head on their parent.

307

Keep talking

By nodding as someone else talks we're saying yes, we're with you, keep going. By nodding slowly or using groups of nods it shows we're listening and engaged.

308

Trust me

Palms open and up signify honesty, openness and that you have nothing to hide. If you're asking or appealing for something it is normal to have your palms up.

309

I'm concentrating really hard

You may have noticed certain people during moments of extreme concentration poking their tongues out very slightly. It has been suggested that this could have developed from a baby's way of saying "I am busy" or "I don't need feeding" and this has carried over into concentrating adults.

I'm interested but something is worrying me a little **30**

With the head rested on finger tips we are likely to be engaged as the weight of our head lies mainly upon our shoulders. The finger tips may just be parked in a self-reassuring face touch.

I'm listening and thinking about how it may affect me **31**

Again the weight of the head is carried by the shoulders so the listener is still engaged. Having the head rested on one finger could however be a clue that the listener is feeling threatened, as the hand and finger protect one side of the vulnerable head.

I'm alert 32

Requiring a degree of flexibility, this kneeling pose may remind us of paying attention at school. It can however take a while to get up and move so also engenders a lack of readiness to act.

I'm interested in what you have to say

33 You're in a group and haven't added anything to the conversation for the first 5 minutes. Finally you pluck up the courage and throw in a comment. It's make or break time. Either the group, and particularly the leader, remain as before, in which case you may as well leave quietly now, or, if they turn to face you… then you have their interest.

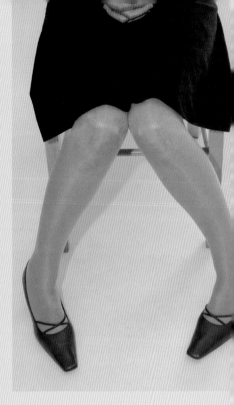

I'm listening and open to you

When wearing skirts and dresses women have few acceptable sitting poses that do not risk a Sharon Stone moment. When leaning forward to listen and seeking rest from the European leg cross, women can either adopt the legs closely clamped together position, or this feet spread pose.

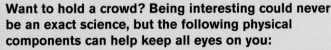

Want to hold a crowd? Being interesting could never be an exact science, but the following physical components can help keep all eyes on you:
- **Eye contact**
- **Facial expressions**
- **Nodding**
- **Appropriate gestures**
- **Engaged posture**

35 Man to man

When in relaxed conversation, one to one, men are more likely to stand at an angle to one another. They associate standing head on with aggression. Women may find this slightly evasive and move to face them whereupon a "dance" may ensue. An exception to this occurs when the man is sexually interested in a female when they may well give them full frontal attention.

Let's talk 36

Men are comfortable sitting at 90 degrees, they do not feel like they are confronting or competing with the other person as they might do when positioned face to face.

Car seat chat

Men are quite happy sitting side by side having a conversation without making great effort to turn and engage the other person; for example when sat side by side in a car. It allows them to avoid facing square on.

Tell me more

Women are less threatened by being face to face with another person; they make less association with aggression and like to engage directly with the other person.

BORED TO TEARS

THINK BACK TO THAT FRIDAY 2PM PHYSICS LESSON AT SCHOOL... HEAD IN HANDS, THE YAWN, DOODLING ENDLESS CIRCLES WITH A HALF CHEWED PEN, ALL THE CLASSIC SIGNS OF BOREDOM...

319 I'm bored

Although you may not be that tired, boredom is almost universally signalled by yawning. This may either be covert, where we make an attempt at concealing it by fighting to keep our eyes open and covering our mouths, or may subconsciously occur quickly followed by an embarrassed apology after a pointed and sarcastic, "Are we keeping you awake?"

320 I need to stretch my rested limbs

Just as we yawn as if tired when bored, stretching is also linked to this sleep related state. It is as if we had just got up in the morning and are stretching our rested limbs.

I need to occupy myself

321

If what we're listening to isn't interesting us, sometimes we have to seek other things to occupy our minds or challenge us… thumb twiddling is just one example.

322

I've forgotten where I am

Occasionally boredom may get to a point where we wander off into daydreams and that's when, forgetting where we are, we publicly display habits usually undertaken in private, such as nose picking.

s someone more interesting going to call me?

323

Either the phone is on silent or they're checking for a new text message. Either way, your sparkling conversation is not currently top of their agenda.

My mind is elsewhere

324

Doodlers may be "listening", but are they really listening and making the communication a two-way process? If they're drawing 23 perfect parallelograms they're probably not hanging on your every word.

325 My mind is someplace else

Imagine going to a bar with your all time hero, be it film or sports star. Would you be slowly pulling the label off your beer bottle as you stare at it thinking of other things? Probably not. When people occupy themselves like this they may be 'listening' but they are just not fully engaged.

When is 326 this going to end?

Looking at the watch: Whether done by subtly pulling back the cuff beneath the table level, or a deliberate stare from the watch to someone else, the message is the same … get on with it!

We've all been at a social gathering when we've been talking to someone and they're looking around, over our shoulders, for something or someone else. Resist the temptation of physical violence and excuse yourself to "find a friend".

ow do I escape this boring person?

I'm somewhere else

Staring into space: When we're really listening we're not just hearing, we're reading the myriad of visual clues. As we tip into boredom however, the eyes stare into space and go into neutral, with the mind sure to follow soon afterwards.

329

This is dull

Arousal and interest is demonstrated by a readiness for action, as this ebbs away the resultant slouching and slumping shows how little you care.

Yawning: Although you may not be that tired, boredom is almost universally signalled by yawning. The other time people may yawn is under conditions of extreme nervousness or stress when it is used as a fill in activity when people are not sure of what else to do.

This clue indicates you're resigned to going nowhere and are stuck with this for the long haul. You are feeling little excitement and are unlikely to get aroused by anything in the near future.

I'm just going to have to put up with this

hy are we waiting

When audiences are kept waiting they may break into a slow hand clap to usher on the show or even to express discontent. Slow handclapping is an ironic imitation of its faster, appreciative cousin!

AROUSAL, EXCITEMENT OR IMPATIENCE

EXCITEMENT REVEALS ITSELF BY READINESS AND MOVEMENT TOWARDS A GOAL.

 **Let's go!**

This ready pose with one foot on its toes shows you're primed for action as it is the position your feet will occupy when you get up.

I'm intent

By leaning forward in the chair, listeners demonstrate a higher level of intent, either to speak or to listen. Either way some relaxation has gone.

I'm excited

"The crowd was on the edge of its seat!" You're watching the last five minutes of the world cup final, the scores are level, and a penalty is awarded. The chances are you're not sitting back coolly watching events; you're preparing yourself to dive in and help out!

335 I want to see

Standing on tip toes is normally reserved for children as a highly practical way of gaining height. As an adult it may be employed to catch someone's attention across a crowded room.

336

I'm engaged with this conversation

When we're relaxed our shoulders drop, pulled down by our arms to our sides and we're happy to allow the back of a chair to take some weight. However, tension and the need to be ready for action make us sit up like a meerkat.

337

I can't wait

Rubbing hands back and forth shows a high degree of excitement or anticipation of something, and that you're happy for everyone to know it.

By rolling up our sleeves we're showing that we're ready for action and are happy to get involved. Although originally a symbol of manual labour, we may still do it in less physical environments to show our willingness to be a team player.

Let's get down to business

I'm ready to contribute

When the hands are on the table it can indicate we have less to hide. We're ready to contribute almost as if it were something physical we are about to undertake rather than a conversation.

DISENGAGEMENT, DISAGREEMENT AND DISINTEREST

WE DON'T AGREE WITH EVERYTHING WE HEAR, NOR ARE WE INTERESTED BY EVERY WORD... AND OUR NON-VERBAL COMMUNICATION NORMALLY MAKES IT CLEAR.

The closed fist could point to a degree of competition or challenge. It may also show lower engagement, not only by the knuckles, but also by the threatening finger.

I want to challenge what's being sai

I disagree with what's being sa

The fist could indicate aggression or a combative attitude. The back of the hand faces the other person, further amplifying a potentially closed viewpoint.

342 This isn't that interesting

Look at the audience at the final of a sporting event, the last night of a great show or a fantastic movie… you're unlikely to find them sitting with their heads supported on their palms.

343

I disagree but won't tell you so

Hands with fingers interwoven may show that the person is keeping themselves in check. The higher the hands are held in this gesture the more defensive and the less open they tend to be.

344

Get on with it

Drumming fingers: Combining rapid movements whilst mimicking feet scurrying away... there can be no doubt that patience is running out.

345 Yes, I hear you and I've got something to say too

Fast nodding urges the current speaker to finish. It conveys that the message has been received and understood and the listener now wants to get their oar in.

This idea is bad, difficult, complicated or tough

346

When we move back in our chair we attempt to physically distance ourselves from an idea that we either don't like or we need to give some serious thought to. It can often be accompanied by a long, deep intake of breath.

347

Head says one thing, body says another

Whilst you may be looking at someone to acknowledge their conversation, your body facing in another direction may give away that your interests lie elsewhere, maybe with other people, maybe with the door!

Get me away from this person

We all seek to move towards the things that we like and away from the things we don't. Even subtly turning the body away can signal disengagement.

You don't warrant a place in our conversation

We find having someone's back turned on us doubly insulting. First, we are written off as not interesting enough to warrant attention, and second we are treated with the contempt of being considered a non-threat and can be safely positioned at our point of weakness.

HOLDING SOMETHING BACK

SOME PEOPLE ARE MORE DIRECT THAN OTHERS, BUT IF WE WENT THROUGH LIFE SAYING EXACTLY WHAT WAS GOING THROUGH OUR HEADS IT WOULD BE A RECIPE FOR DISASTER. WE HAVE BECOME SKILLED AT NOT BLURTING OUT EVERY THOUGHT, BUT SOMETIMES OUR BODY LANGUAGE TELLS OTHERS WE'VE GOT SOMETHING ON OUR MINDS.

350

I'm being careful about what I say

When we talk, our hands talk; try asking an Italian to say anything with his hands behind his back. Torture. One way of not giving the game away is to tuck your hands under the table. Try it.

I'm closed to the idea but won't tell you

The cross of the body already represents a barrier but by grasping the arms

351

we are conveying that we're physically holding ourselves back, either from saying or from doing something.

352 I'm listening but really I want to speak myself

Have you ever seen someone with their hand over their mouth as they listen to you? This signal could be them physically trying to inhibit themselves from commenting. They may have something to say... perhaps you should ask them?

353 I'm not interested and I'm not going to let you know

If someone is covering their mouth and resting their head on their hand, it's likely, they're not interested, but what's worse is they aren't going to let you know it; in fact, they're physically stopping themselves.

I'm holding 354
myself back here

Almost as if we're stopping ourselves from being torn out of the chair, here the hands tightly grip the armrests to restrain ourselves from leaping into action.

355 I'm playing
no part in this

If you watch a film of a group of people in conversation with the sound turned down, it is often possible to identify who is talking purely on the basis of who is gesturing. If someone is sitting on their hands it often indicates a lack of intent to participate in the debate. They've "checked out".

You sexy thing.

SO MUCH OF OUR MODERN DAY BODY LANGUAGE IS DRIVEN BY ONE OF OUR MOST POTENT AND BASIC DESIRES... SEX.

Making ourselves appealing to the opposite sex is frequently achieved by drawing attention to our physical gender differences. We can all use non-verbal communication to make ourselves more attractive.

BUYING SIGNS AND FLIRTING

MEN FREQUENTLY COMPLAIN, "WHY DO WE ALWAYS HAVE TO MAKE THE FIRST MOVE?" ALTHOUGH THE APPROACH IS TYPICALLY THE MAN'S, THE WOMAN HAS FREQUENTLY BEEN SENDING A WHOLE RAFT OF 'FIRST MOVES' IN TERMS OF HER NON-VERBAL COMMUNICATION. MAYBE MEN SHOULD JUST TRY TO GET AS GOOD AS WOMEN AT READING THE CLUES.

356 You look interesting

The foot point: People often seek to reduce the distance between themselves and people they like. Subconsciously this is sometimes given away when our feet, in either a legs crossed or standing position, point towards a person we like or find attractive.

Come closer 357

The knee point: Sometimes when we're sitting we'll indicate our liking for someone by pointing our knee in their direction. This closes the distance between them and us. This is often combined with a foot tucked under the buttock or thigh.

Checking you out

When sizing up a member of the opposite sex we'll often look them up and down as we search for desirable or undesirable characteristics. These could include facial attractiveness, weight, height, posture and physique, or could be 'adornments' such as clothes, or the absence of an engagement or wedding ring to indicate suitability and availability.

I'm interested

Each of us may have a different sense of what we consider our "personal space". It's a potential buying sign when someone moves markedly into your space or doesn't back off as you subtly reduce the distance between you.

360

Get your eyes off me

Maybe you're coming on a bit too strong… When a woman is uncomfortable with your degree of attention she may seek to cover up and shut you out. One way of doing this is to cover exposed flesh, such as the wrists, by pulling her sleeves down.

Dancing cheek to cheek: In body language terms, closeness is often a metaphor for liking. A classic illustration of this is dancing close to a member of the opposite sex. This can be witnessed in slow or fast dancing when flirting couples will close to much shorter distances than the regular cultural norm.

361 Try me, I'm new and different

People sitting this way are attempting to convey their individuality or difference. The iconic 1960s' photograph of Christine Keeler, of Profumo Affair fame, is an archetypal example.

362 Undress me

The shoe fondle can either take the form of taking the shoe on and off to simulate sexual penetration, or the caressing of the shoe and foot as a substitute phallus.

363 I want to get close to you

Pulling a chair towards someone could be a conscious effort to hold attention, or could be a subconscious result of enjoying someone's flirting

364 I'd like to get to know you better

Can you imagine caressing or stroking a work colleague or best friend? It's pretty unlikely. Caressing is mostly reserved for intimate, sexual situations.

HELLO BOYS

FROM AN EVOLUTIONARY STANDPOINT, WOMEN NEED TO DISPLAY THAT THEY ARE GOOD POTENTIAL BABY MAKING MACHINES IN ORDER TO ATTRACT MEN. WHAT DOES THIS MEAN? TYPICALLY THEY MUST BE AVAILABLE (NOT 'TAKEN' BY ANOTHER MALE), NOT PREGNANT ALREADY, YOUNG, FIT AND HEALTHY. EXERCISE EXTREME CAUTION WHEN TRYING TO PICK UP THESE CLUES, IF IN DOUBT ERR ON THE SIDE OF CAUTION… AND NEVER ASSUME ONE NON-VERBAL CLUE ON ITS OWN IS A COME ON.

365 I want to touch you

The accidental touch: Different people have different levels of tactile comfort. When a woman keeps brushing past or touching you it could mean that she likes you.

366 Look how female I am

Jennifer Lopez's buttocks have achieved global notoriety and have become her trademark. Men have found women's bottoms attractive from the time when they were a display of sexual readiness.

367

The past few years have seen a growth in fashion of crop tops and pierced belly buttons, but why do men find a flat stomach attractive? Genetically there can be nothing more off putting than mating with a female who has already been impregnated by a rival. So today men have evolved to find the opposite of a pregnant belly attractive.

I'm not pregnant and in condition to breed

368 Care for m

Much footage of Princess Diana shows her in this pose with her head down yet looking up. She was an expert in employing this child like posture which helped create a huge wave of sympathy for her.

Look at my mouth

Running the tongue over the teeth does two things for a woman… firstly it ensures removal of any rogue lipstick, but secondly it draws attention to one of the most sensual and alluring parts of a woman's body, the lips.

ouch me like this

Dress smoothing may be just an excuse for self touching. Self-stroking or caressing could be too blatant, whereas dress smoothing sends the same signal in a slightly subtler form.

Look at my wet lips

Licking lips: Women accentuate their lips not only by pushing them out to make them appear full, but also by licking them wet, subconsciously mirroring the appearance of the vagina.

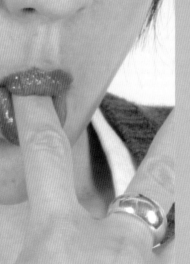

372

Sexy mouth

Finger licking by women is highly arousing to men. Not only does the finger mimic a penis, it draws attention to the lips while simultaneously wetting them.

Sexy lips

3 3

The pout: A huge global industry exists to emphasise and colour women's lips. Human lips are unusual in being pushed out and it has been suggested they have evolved like this to deliberately mimic the vaginal lips. Thus, by pouting, a woman brings attention to the lips as a focal point for the man.

3 4

Fluttering eyes

Many items of a woman's make up are designed to highlight the eyes, make them look bigger and thus more attractive to men. By fluttering their eyelashes, women attempt to draw attention to their eyes. Plucking or raising the eyebrows can also add to the overall effect.

375

Look at my silky, young hair

Hair flicking: It is women who most frequently acknowledge and react to attention, such as a glance in the street, by flicking their hair. Drawing attention to shiny, thick hair – associated with youth and health, suggests they are a good potential mother. They know you're watching!

Look how thick my hair is

376

Hair ruffling: As we age our hair inevitably becomes thinner. Women ruffle their hair to emphasize its volume, and thus youthfulness, to men.

37 Look at my hair

Sometimes practicality demands keeping hair back and out of the way, but often this grooming action continues when the hair is perfectly under control… simply to draw attention. This happens most often when the hair is young and thick, reflecting her youth.

38 Showing off long hair

Lois Lane, sitting at her desk at the *Daily Planet*; pencil skirt, thick rimmed glasses, hair up in a "bun". Often women may de-sexualize themselves in order to be taken seriously at work. But let the hair down with a shake of the head, preferably in slow motion, and the men are drooling.

379 Run your hands through my hair!

Potentially a clear sexual signal, a woman draws attention to the femininity of her long hair with an act that only she or a lover is likely to perform.

380

Look how resilien my hair is

For our distant ancestors, grooming ourselves would have been an important activity to keep ourselves clean and free from parasites. Although this necessity may have gone, we still see its legacy in the form of hair twirling and other hair manipulating activities.

381 Check out my legs

Legs are of considerable sexual interest to a man. It has been suggested by Desmond Morris and others that the reason is the relative lengthening that happens to a female's legs during puberty which coincides with her readiness to bare children.

382

Have you seen my legs?

Crossing and uncrossing legs whilst sat draws attention to the legs and may help lure men into a woman's web.

383

Look down here

This action attracts a man's eyes to the leg and, using a foot to rub the leg, mimics a caressing hand.

384

The leg twine highlights the difference between the frequently slimmer and less heavily muscled female leg.

My legs are not like a man's

385

Maybe you could stroke my leg?

When a woman strokes her leg she may be suggesting that she wants to be stroked there by a nearby man. The stroke is an intimate form of touching.

386

Have you noticed how slender my legs are?

Men rarely sit with the two lower legs parallel and crossed and thus find it very attractive.

387

Look how long my legs are

By sitting on the floor, legs bent and folded to one side a woman makes them appear longer and more alluring to men.

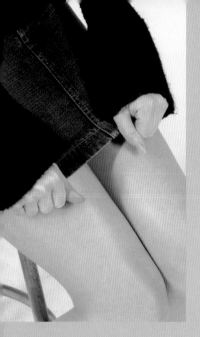

388

Green light or red ligh

As with almost every clue, the act of tugging the skirt to cover the legs needs to be read in the context of other clues and the environment. It could be genuine discomfort with unwanted attention or quite the reverse. By employing this movement the woman could be deliberately advertising the exposed flesh of her legs.

389

Maybe you could touch my thigh?

A woman touching herself can be one of the most erotic acts for a man. Witnessing a woman stroking her thigh evokes in a man the desire to do it for her. This may be a subconscious signal that the woman wishes to be touched there.

390
Neck on show

When seeking to attract men, the amount of flesh on show can be an indicator of availability. By elongating the neck to bring more attention to it, women can make themselves more alluring.

391
Now look at my neck

Touching the neck directs a man's gaze to an area where an amount of naked flesh may be exposed.

392 Have you notice my sensuous neck?

When receiving attention, a woman may indicate it's not entirely unwanted with this clue. By playing with her earring she shows her neck to the man. Alternatively, she may just be easing tension.

393

Check out my hips and waist

The hip tilt is difficult or impossible for a man to adopt and draws attention to the difference in ratio between a man's waist and hips and a woman's. Consequently men find it an alluring pose.

394 Hippy chick

Where the hip tilt is a blatant way of showing female sexuality and gender difference. A more subtle way to direct attention to the hips is to place just one hand on the waist, drawing the eye to the hip curve and ratio.

I'm all 395 feminine curves

Take a look at the red carpet stance of many film stars. Often they're adopting a coquettish pose, glancing over their own shoulder. Doing this draws attention to the roundness of the shoulder echoing the breast and the buttock.

396 **I'm playful**

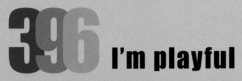

Legs crossed, shoe playfully balanced on a woman's toes. This display of the foot is not day-to-day behaviour. Her comfort with exposing more than the norm indicates an acceptance of attention and could suggest that she may like to remove more than the shoe.

397

Check out the way I move

Picture a procession of supermodels swaying their way down the catwalk. The rolling hips walk achieves two things. Firstly, it accentuates the different hip to waist ratio of men and women; secondly, a man's physiology just doesn't allow him to "swing those hips" in the same way. It's the combination of these two factors which make a woman's walk so attractive to men.

398

You caught me looking

The sideways look clue is frequently grouped with a sight smile and a raise of the closer eyebrow. The flirtation comes from the suggested intimacy and secrecy of the look which is an attempt to send a signal without others noticing.

399

If you're lucky this could be you

Stroking and caressing are motions inextricably linked with courtship and sex. By stroking your wineglass you are suggesting sex.

400

Do I know what I'm doing?

Taking a ring on and off could be an unconscious mannerism, but the danger is that this clue could be read as a blatant allusion to sexual penetration.

401

I really like you

It has been suggested that the origin of the deep tongue kiss is a time before super convenient baby foods, where a mother may have masticated food for an infant to digest. To that end the kiss could be a throwback to a baby's tongue searching its mother's mouth for food.

402 I want to communicate with you physically as well as verbally

Some people are just more tactile than others. For this to be a real clue, watch and see if everyone is afforded a warm platonic touch. If it's just you, it could be a clue that the person would like to get a lot more intimate with you.

403 Hello boys

Humans have disproportionately large breasts, larger than necessary to fulfil the needs of feeding. It has been suggested that the reason is that the breasts mimic the buttocks, which have long been the signal or invitation for sex. By displaying cleavage, the subconscious sexual connection and urge is triggered in men.

404 Look at my chest

By tightening upper body clothing a woman more clearly outlines her breasts and reinforces their round, buttock echoing form.

405

Have you noticed my young breasts?

Firm breasts are associated with youth and therefore a higher ability to produce children. Using the arms, a woman may physically push up her breasts to simulate this firmness.

406

I'm all woman

Women have a tendency to have their wrists limp, or cocked, often with the hand towards their bodies. Men rarely rest in this position, though some gay men take on this attribute to complement their sexuality.

Look at my exposed, feminine flesh

The wrist display: When a woman makes a deliberate move to expose a greater amount of flesh it may well be a clue that she is trying to generate attention. By exposing the frequently covered wrists she could be offering a taste of things to come.

408 I even smo[ke] femininely

The almost exclusively female trait of the wrist cock to expose extra flesh can be convenient device for women smokers to advertise their femininity.

409

This is how I look when I make love

Mastered by Marilyn Monroe, the drooping eyelid display is said to mimic female orgasmic expressions, thereby arousing males.

HELLO LADIES

IN MODERN TIMES A WOMAN MAY BE ATTRACTED BY MEN WHO CAN OFFER STABILITY, FINANCIAL SECURITY AND A CARING HOME LIFE. HOWEVER WHEN MATING AND DATING, WOMEN ARE STILL DRIVEN BY A MORE PRIMEVAL DESIRE FOR A STRONG, DOMINANT MAN WHO WOULD BE ABLE TO DEFEND THE FAMILY GROUP.

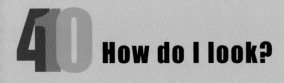

40 How do I look?

Just like David Brent in *The Office*, the man adjusting his tie to check and straighten his appearance is partaking in pure preening.

41 I like your bottom

The buttocks hold particular interest for a man as they would typically have been his mating view in earlier evolutionary states. If he can't resist touching he may cheekily try the bottom smack.

42 You've got a great ass

As Italian as the Vespa, pizza and Rome, the bottom pinch was for generations a sign of appreciation of a woman. Using this old tradition in modern times could land you in jail!

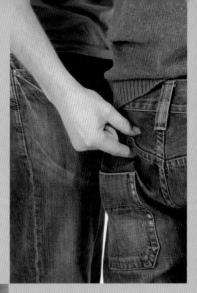

43 I'm a powerful masculine ma

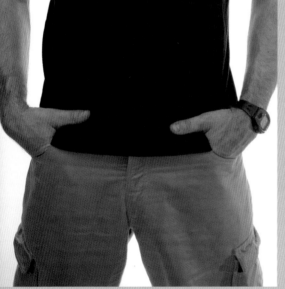

Here the hands point to the groin, indicating the sexual organ. The thumbs, being the power digit, amplify the gesture by signifying dominance.

My masculinity is definitely on show

44

The hands may be pushed all the way into the trousers or shorts, or it might be just the fingers. Either way it's a classic crotch show.

Look how strong I am

45

A woman's more primeval urges cause her to be attracted to strong healthy males who are likely to be able to protect them and their offspring. One marker of this is chest and arm strength, which men may display in t-shirts or tank tops.

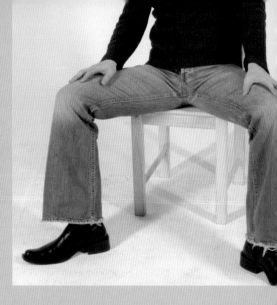

Check out my masculinity

This classic "bloke" posture exhibits high levels of relaxation whilst being a blatant show of masculinity.

Look how much testosterone I produ

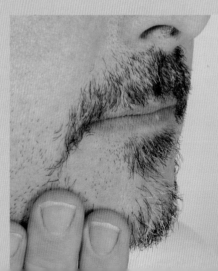

Originally serving a hygiene function, grooming facial hair also attracts attention to this symbol of a man's masculinity.

48 Look down here

A classic cowboy stance in which the hands point towards the groin in a crotch display and the thumbs hitch in the pockets. At the same time the elbows are pushed out to increase the man's overall size.

49 I'm big and not afraid to flaunt my masculinity

In this pose, the hands direct attention towards the man's groin. This is as close as we'll come to a full sexual organ display in public. Pushing the elbows out also has the effect of making him look bigger.

420 I'm the king of the bar

A man in this pose is cranking up his dominance in two ways... the relaxation says he's happy to leave his torso unprotected, whilst the elbows on the bar create a pair of super shoulders of his upper arms. He could be the group leader, happy to adopt a relaxed pose while others are forced to stand.

421

Men have few inhibitions about adjusting themselves in public, compared to a woman. Especially seen amongst groups of men, such as sports teams, they are making straightforward sexual displays.

Check out my package

4 22 Curves in all the right places

Using the hands to outline the hourglass figure of a woman is beloved by builders when watching a curvy young lady pass by, and it may be further supported by a wolf whistle. It focuses on describing some of the key areas of difference between male and female bodies, indicating breasts, hips and buttocks.

4 23 Look how pumped up and strong I am

Men who spend too much time in the gym shifting unfeasible weights can't resist drawing attention to their exaggerated bodies by puffing out their chests and holding their arms at an angle to their bodies in the "body builder walk". Most women know that muscle mass is often inversely proportional to IQ. Sorry, Arnold.

PARTNERSHIP

IN THE MAIN, MAN HAS EVOLVED INTO A MONOGAMOUS SPECIES WHERE ONE MALE PAIRS WITH ONE FEMALE. THOUGH BREAKING DOWN WITH THE RISE IN SINGLE PARENT FAMILIES, THE 'STANDARD' UNIT REMAINS ONE MAN TO ONE WOMAN, AND MANY OF OUR ASPECTS OF NON-VERBAL COMMUNICATION ADVERTISE OUR TIES TO EACH OTHER.

424 We're together

Holding hands leaves no one in any doubt that this couple is off the market. It's like writing 'property of' on each person. At the same time it reassures both parties in the same way as a parent's caring hand reassures a child.

425 You're mine

Having your arm around someone's waist is a show of protection and caring or of a connection between two people, but can also be seen as a mark of ownership.

I trust **426** you to care for me

Having someone over our shoulder like a teacher standing behind us at school puts us ill at ease. But we allow our lovers to embrace us from the point of our greatest weakness.

427 We belong to each other

Walking arm in arm serves several purposes. It provides the comfort of contact, and it indicates to other parties (and potential mates) that we are unavailable. It can also be a display of a "trophy" partner, particularly where there is a marked difference in the age, desirability or attractiveness of the pair.

428 I really trust y[ou]

We identify adults feeding each other as lovers. The only other occasion adults would be likely to feed each other would be in the context of injury or sickness. Each of those situations demands trust and closeness.

429 Lean on me

Resting our head on someone else's shoulder fulfils the practical need for a pillow but also reminds us of resting our head against a parent's body as a child.

430 She's my girl

Sitting on someone's lap is most often seen with a child on a parent's knee or a woman on a man's. We rarely observe this with genders reversed or in same sex situations. For the female it may remind her of childhood comforts, whilst for the man it reinforces his dominance.

431 We love each other

Arms around each other: Imagine two lovers on a romantic walk in Central Park on a summer's evening with their arms around each other. This is an ownership display by both parties but at the same time both partners are receiving the reassurance afforded by the maximum degree of body contact achievable whilst walking together.

432

I'm with them

Our heads are highly sensitive parts of our bodies which we seek to protect and keep a safe distance from harm's way. Consequently, head touching represents a position of high trust in the other person and is normally reserved for partners or close family.

Under pressure.

WHEN WE RECEIVE
EXTERNAL STIMULI
THAT UNBALANCE
US IT TRIGGERS
STRESS,
TENSION

and an excess of nervous energy, which may reveal itself in a huge variety of physical ways. When we experience this heightened level of tension we often seek to reassure ourselves.

DISCOMFORT, TENSION AND PRESSURE INDICATORS

WE ARE SUBJECTED TO A MULTITUDE OF TENSIONS AND STRESSES EVERY DAY OF OUR LIVES. THEY MANIFEST THEMSELVES IN A MULTITUDE OF WAYS THAT WE ARE HIGHLY TUNED TO PICK UP IN OTHERS.

There's too much attention on me

As the pressure rises, the rate at which we blink increases dramatically.

434

I'm highly self conscious

Asked to perform something that makes us highly self conscious, for example, speaking in public, may bring some people out in blotchy rashes on the neck.

435

I'm shaking like a leaf

The actor before the first night performance, the player before the cup final and the groom waiting anxiously at the altar; all know too well that the "shakes" announce pretty serious nerves.

436 Under pressure

Swallowing is a subconscious act most of the time in our day to day lives. When the pressure is on however, we may become more self conscious and the rate at which we swallow may jump.

I'm feeling the "heat"

Here we're talking nervous sweating rather than reaction to heat. Our body automatically kicks in to help cool us down before we're called to some physical challenge. These days it's more likely to be confronting a hostile audience than beating off a sabre toothed tiger!

I need to calm myself

When all eyes are on us, we can get so uptight that we start taking short, rapid breaths, or even momentarily stop breathing all together. It all becomes too much and at a some point we need to take one really long, deep breath.

 **I couldn't be more tense**

As we relax, tension escapes from our bodies. Soldiers are made to stand to attention when being inspected to indicate that their lower status does not permit them to be relaxed. When we feel ourselves under the microscope we may also adopt rather more rigid postures and poses.

 My ears are burning

As blood rushes to the surface of our skin our ears can burn. There's not much you can do about this, short of growing your hair long!

 I'm embarrassed

When you've been caught doing something you shouldn't have been doing, or are feeling extremely self conscious, most people blush. When it starts, there's nothing you can do to stop it.

442

I'm not relaxed

As the pressure goes on, we often hunch up our shoulders. Tension draws the body in on itself, hunching the shoulders, tightening the posture and simulating a defensive position.

443

I'm feeling a bit self conscious

New, unfamiliar social situations create a degree of unease in all of us. This reveals itself as we take nervous non-sips of our drink.

444

I'm feeling uneasy

The need to work off tension or stress is rendered more difficult when seated. However, the desire can still surface in shifting movements with no purpose in a chair, sometimes resulting in an even more uncomfortable position.

445

Hot under the collar

The effect of nerves can raise the body's temperature and increase sweating and irritability of the neck, causing someone under pressure to attempt to "let off some steam".

My mouth has dried up

Lip smacking: High levels of anxiety can cause the mouth to dry up. By swallowing and smacking the lips the mouth can be "oiled up" before trying to speak.

I feel like moving

We may be having a conversation or in another situation where we can't leave. This discomfort may make us roll onto the outside of our feet, achieving movement without our feet leaving the spot.

TENSION RELEASES

Pressure, nerves, worry, and embarrassment – in our modern lives we're subjected to many stresses but often can't act directly against the cause. If you watch carefully you can see we've developed a variety of pressure release valves to let off steam.

I've got tension to walk off 448

Imagine the scene at a hospital waiting room as an anxious parent awaits the end of an operation on their child. Racked with worry but helpless to assist, the stress is alleviated by incessant pacing. Pacing without meaning can also be the hallmark of the anxious presenter.

449 I want to move

When seated with the "European leg cross", tension is sometimes released by the rhythmic bouncing of the balanced leg. This echoes the rhythm of being rocked as a child.

I've got surplus nervous energy built up inside

When sat in one place, perhaps working at a desk all day, the pressure can mount up. We can't move around to dissipate it so how do we leak the energy? By jiggling the foot nervously up and down.

I'm stressed and tired

You're dog tired and confronted by a seemingly endless pile of things to do and a mountainous in-tray. This pained expression and frantic rubbing of the forehead by the thumb and finger tips may release some stress, but it's not going to make the workload go away.

I need a fiddle

An abbreviated version of nail biting, this is one of the commonest tension releases as the hands pick and stroke the nails and surrounding skin. Next time you're on a train or bus, watch people's hands as they idly tug at their fingers.

I'm stirred up inside

Perhaps you've worked or sat next to someone who does this…an incessant foot tapping or knee jumping as the heel repeatedly goes up and down. Inner excitement or nervousness is, in some part, soothed and alleviated in these movements.

I need to do something

One way of releasing tension is nail biting. We may gain additional comfort from nail biting by the self touch of the lips which occurs at the same time.

I'll take it out on the gum

Chewing gums may be flavoured, however our compulsive and vigorous chewing goes on long after the taste has gone. Potentially an adult substitute for thumb sucking, potentially a relic of more continuous grazing habits, gum can help relieve pressure. Just take a look at harassed sports managers and coaches who can't intervene in the game.

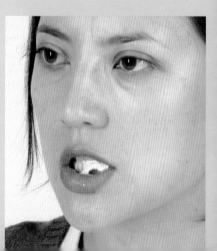

456

This makes noise and releases my tension

Jangling keys or coins in a pocket can be very distracting. This tension release may be an indicator of a desire to leave as the keys are prepared for the car or door.

457

Jewellery fondling

Body adornments such as bracelets and necklaces provide the perfect outlet for nervous energy as they are constantly adjusted and readjusted.

458

I want to move

Swivelling a chair may be looking for a way out or releasing pent up tension; either way, sitting stock still is not an option. It also reminds us of the rocking movement we received as a child which continues to reassure us as an adult.

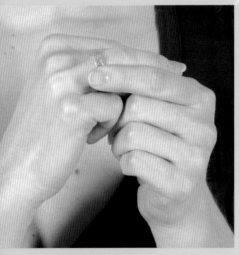

459

Hamster in a whee

Ring turning can provide an endless source of tension release. Rather like a hamster wheel, there's no end to the movement of the ring; it can turn and turn and turn...

I'm keyed up

The drink doesn't need stirring but we still turn and re-examine the contents of the glass to distract ourselves.

'll move this around

As with many ways of leaking nervous energy, glass shifting deliberately involves a third party object onto which the tension can be offloaded or displaced.

GAINING REASSURANCE AND REASSURING OTHERS

FROM THE MOMENT WE EMERGE FROM OUR MOTHER'S WOMB WE SEEK THE SANCTITY OF REASSURANCE. MOST OF THE WAYS THAT OUR BODY LANGUAGE DELIVERS THIS REASSURANCE ARE DERIVED FROM THE SAME SIMPLE COMFORTS WE WERE AFFORDED BY OUR CARERS WHEN WE WERE CHILDREN.

462 I want my Mummy

Usually abandoned as we grow up, thumb sucking is the most blatant substitute for the reassurance and comfort gained from sucking a mother's nipple. The child is normally not hungry, but is trying to recreate the security associated with this act.

463 I'm comforted

Even though it has burnt out half an hour ago, Grandpa still sits back sucking his pipe. Like a simple dummy, at some level smokers are comforted by the physical contact against their lips.

Comfort me

Here, by pinching the bottom lip we attempt to recreate the reassurance afforded by the mother's breast, perhaps as we weigh up a difficult or troubling situation.

Am I OK?

When a child breast feeds, the upper lip may be pushed up. Touching this area as an adult may bring those warm feelings flooding back.

466

That's calming me

When we are considering options, and someone's attention is upon us, we can feel ill at ease. To cope with this the arm of a pair of glasses can be the perfect prop.

467

My dummy replacement

Pen sucking is another surrogate nipple habit which remains with some for the whole of their lives.

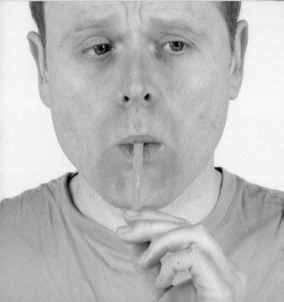

468

I'm being led in the right direction

We don't always display our insecurities face to face. By grasping our arms behind our back we are giving ourselves the reassuring guiding hold of an adult leading and protecting us.

469

Reassure me

There are few things more natural than the sight of a parent leading the child by the hand. The hand supports the child, keeps them safe and guides them in the right direction. When we're alone in the big, bad world our parent is gone; holding a work colleague's hand is plainly inappropriate so we do the next best thing – we hold our own hands.

470

Secretly, I need reassurance

By holding our hand behind our back, we achieve reassurance whilst masking the self comforting gesture.

I want someone to embrace me

In this pose we come as close as we can to embracing another person, by drawing our heels in and treating our doubled up legs as a mock person who can reassure us.

Men rarely sit with one leg tucked under their thigh or buttock, but it is a pose which makes the person feel comforted by the pressing of body against foot. It may also form a knee point towards someone or something in which they are interested.

472 I feel cradled and reassured

473

I feel for you

When our emotions are stirred by someone else, sitting and listening is often not enough. We feel the need to close the distance and, by putting a hand on theirs, to offer the reassurance of physical contact.

Are you sure that's right ?

IT IS OFTEN SAID THAT YOU CAN'T BELIEVE EVERYTHING THAT COMES OUT OF SOMEONE'S MOUTH, and we have many ways of conveying our uncertainty or lack of faith. Body language can offer clues to work out whether someone is convinced by what is being said… but never jump to the conclusion the speaker is lying on the evidence of just one clue.

CONTEMPLATING AND CONSIDERING

W E CAN'T ALWAYS MAKE OUR MINDS UP INSTANTLY; WE OFTEN NEED A LITTLE TIME TO WEIGH UP THE OPTIONS AND WORK OUT OUR RESPONSE, TO WHAT WE'RE HEARING.

44 Let me think about that

Rather like Rodin's statue, The Thinker, this is a classic indication that someone is weighing up options. When they stop, the decision may have been made.

45 I dunno

Almost as if we are trying to stir the brain into activity, the head scratch is a classic indication that we're struggling with something.

I'll decide about that **476**

The evaluative "steepling" gesture of the hands conveys confidence, control and superiority. Caution should be applied to its use to avoid the appearance of arrogance.

I want to make a **477** point

Whilst the grasped and interlocked fingers convey that the speaker is holding themselves in check, the steepled index fingers signal that that they have a point to make.

I'm not sure if I agree

Used in non-religious contexts, this gesture conveys direction and closed mindedness as the hands are 'closed' and the palms hidden from view. The person is unlikely to be listening to you.

I'm still thinking

A classic thinking pose, it is likely that the person is both listening and evaluating.

480

Let me see

When we examine something, we often squint to catch the minute detail, so as we contemplate something we often reproduce the same expression to examine the intangible.

481

I'm thinking it over

When we're chewing something over we may gently stroke the underside of our chins from back to front.

I'm sizing this up

As someone defensively considers what we're saying, they may subconsciously keep their head and neck protectively down until they accept and look up or disagree and look away.

483

Either one or the other

Rocking the head from side to side: It's as if moving the head will allow you to view options from different angles, perhaps signalling a process of selection between two options.

484

That needs thinking about

Pursed lips can often be associated with evaluation, especially when accompanied with a furrowed brow and gazing upwards, as if searching for an answer.

STALLING FOR TIME

SOMETIMES, WE ALL NEED TO BUY OURSELVES SOME TIME IN ORDER TO FIND A WAY OF BROACHING A DIFFICULT SUBJECT OR OTHERWISE EXTRACTING OURSELVES FROM A SITUATION.

Ummmm 485

Even though no fluff is present, people still pick at it. Perhaps they're just stalling for time as they try to work out what to say. Alternatively they may be shy and looking for a way to "release" their embarrassment.

486 Well...

With no other physical activity or object to divert your attention onto, you make the easiest move possible to introduce a distraction between you and your interrogator. By bringing your hand up and examining your fingernails, you're hoping to offload some of the attention onto your hands as you desperately seek an answer...

487 Hmmm...

Glasses provide a useful device for releasing surplus nervous tension. Regardless of whether they need cleaning or not, they at least give a precious few moments to work out your course of action.

488 How should I put this...

Adjusting glasses: In an attempt to find anything to do rather than answer a question, the glasses wearer has a distinct advantage with a ready made prop.

489

Something in my eye

By feigning something in the eye, it is not only possible to gain an extra few seconds (in the same way as you may do by clearing your throat), but it also breaks eye contact and lessens the pressure exerted by the other party waiting for your answer!

POSSIBLE LYING INDICATORS

Below you'll find some of the clues to lying. There is no foolproof way of using body language to uncover deceit, but some of the following may help depending on the environment and other clues present.

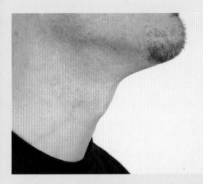

490

Nervous swallowing: More easily identified in men than women due to the size of the Adam's apple, raised levels of nervous swallowing may mean something is being hidden.

I'm self conscious about what I say

491 Stop these words coming out

Covering our mouths while talking is almost as if we are trying to stop ourselves saying things we know to be untrue. More generally, hand to mouth gestures as we speak may send the signal that there's some chicanery going on, or nervousness about what we're saying.

492

I'm not happy looking at you as I say this

We just don't trust people with shifty eyes. It's particularly noticeable when someone is listening to you as this is normally when levels of eye contact would be at their highest. Sometimes, liars compensate by overplaying eye contact, staring instead of making natural contact at the beginning and end of statements.

493

The eye rub may be employed in an attempt to shut out the other person by cutting off your eyes from view to prevent them "reading" you.

I don't want to see your reaction

My eyes might give me away

494

Just like the eye rub, we abbreviate the movement of covering our eyes, but our intent, to avoid giving away our lie with the eyes, is the same.

495

Lying with a smile

We can spot falseness a mile off – despite the smile, the top half of the face remains impassive and the eyes empty.

496 I'm nervous about saying this

Famously present during President Clinton's denials of the Monica Lewinsky affair, the nose touch is thought to be a close relation to the mouth cover, where the hand comes up to cover the mouth but instead goes to touch the nose.

497

The nose rub is just like the nose touch; when being economical with the truth we just can't stop touching our face.

I'm anxious about what I'm saying

498 My hands may give me away

Impassive hands: A study by Desmond Morris showed that the amount of gestures used by people reduces when they are lying. Perhaps they are afraid their hands will give them away?

499

I don't like what I'm saying

In the same way as we may physically cover our mouths to stop lies, we may also try to cover our ears to prevent hearing the deceit. Stopping short of covering them, we end up tugging our ears instead.

There is a rise in the incidence of the "hand shrug" gesture when lying, potentially because the speaker is making over eager appeals for our belief.

500

Please believe me

Index

Acknowledgements

This book is the sum of collective efforts and wisdom of a number of people. I'd like to express my thanks and gratitude to the following people who contributed, directly or indirectly through their ideas, inspiration, help or coaching, to the creation of
The Body Language Phrasebook:

Victoria Alers-Hankey, Chris Stone, Guy Hearn, Desmond Morris, Albert Mehrabian, Richard Bandler, John Grinder, Paul Ekman, Virginia Satir, Geoffrey Beattie, Jill Danks, Jane Endacott, Scott Edgerton-Black, Saskia Martyn-David, Carmel Van Den Bergh, Anna Raine, Elissa Telfer, Tim Baynes, Neil Flett, Peter Rogen, Milton Erickson, Anthony Robbins, Herb Cohen, Phil Clucas.